Parl

in

The Peak

CH00728731

Parkes
in
The Peak

Ted Parkes

The Pentland Press Ltd.
Edinburgh · Cambridge · Durham

©A E Parkes 1993

First published in 1993 by
The Pentland Press Ltd.
1 Hutton Close
South Church
Durham

All rights reserved. Unauthorised duplication contravenes existing laws.

ISBN 1 85821 097 6

Printed in Great Britain by BPCC Wheatons Ltd, Exeter

Acknowledgements

My grateful thanks go to Sandy Matthews for his support and encouragement, for the many hours spent in the word processing and layout of the walks, and his help in the production of the maps.

Thanks also to Sandy's daughter, Karen, who willingly gave up part of her Christmas vacation to assist in the word processing.

To my son-in-law, Andrew Haworth, go my thanks for his suggestion of the title for the book.

Ted Parkes

The route maps are based upon the Ordnance Survey map with the sanction of
The Controller of HM Stationery Office.

Cover Pictures

Front: The famous millstone symbol of the Peak District National Park
- this particular one located near the village of Thorpe.

Back: One of the author's favourite spots - Washgate Bridge near
Hollinsclough (see Walks 16 and 19).

Photographs by Sandy Matthews

Introduction

The name 'Peak District' probably conjures up a picture of a landscape dominated by craggy hilltops, whereas the reality is very different (its highest points are, in fact, the peaty plateaus of Bleaklow and Kinder).

Peak District is from the Old English word *peac* - 'knoll, hill, peak' - and in the seventh century Tribal Hidage (land taxes) there is reference to '*pecsætna lond*', the land of the settlers of the Peak (hill dwellers), of whom there were 1,200 households.

Also, in the Anglo-Saxon Chronicles of AD 924, Bakewell is said to be in 'peac lond'.

The whole area is justifiably famous for the magnificence and variety of its scenery, attested by the 18-20 million people who visit it each year.

Criss-crossed as it is with a multitude of public footpaths and rights of way, most of which are well maintained and signed, the whole area is a ramblers' paradise.

Indeed, on foot is the only way to explore and appreciate this magnificent countryside of wooded river dales, dry dales with beautiful flowers, limestone uplands, gritstone edges and heather covered moorlands, all inset with attractive and interesting villages and hamlets.

Where to go, how to find your way around and what to look for?

These were the questions asked of me by a small group of would-be ramblers in the 40's-50's age group with little or no previous experience of rambling.

The 35 walks in the book are a selection I devised for them as an introduction to a wide cross-section of what the Peak District has to offer.

So well received were they that I was encouraged to offer them to a wider public; hence the book.

All the walks are circular, the majority averaging 9-10 miles in length, a reasonable distance for a pleasant day's outing. Most are arranged to have a relatively easy finish.

I have not attempted to give a time duration for the individual walks since there are too many variables, such as number and ability of walkers, number and length of refreshment stops, sightseeing time, weather, terrain and so forth.

As a guide, the group I have mentioned averaged, overall, 1½ to 2 miles per hour, i.e. 4½ to 6 hours for a nine mile walk.

Route instructions are given in great detail, and, together with the accompanying maps, should ensure satisfactory completion of the walks without getting lost. I do, however, strongly recommend taking along the appropriate OS map(s) as an insurance against the eventuality of becoming 'misplaced'. There is also the bonus of the additional information given on the maps.

The text includes references to pubs, shops, tea rooms and public toilets, but it should be remembered that opening times can vary with season and day of the week. Background information on points and places of interest is given at the end of each walk.

For those unfamiliar with grid references, full explanations can be found on both Outdoor Leisure Maps Nos. 1 and 24. Here is a simple example:-

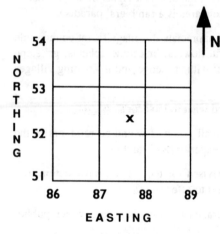

In any grid reference the easting is always quoted first.

Take figures of grid line west of square containing point **X**, i.e. 87; estimate tenths between this line and point **X**, i.e. 7.

Therefore easting reference = 877.

Take figures of grid line south of square containing point **X**, i.e. 52; estimate tenths between this line and point **X**, i.e. 3.

Therefore northing reference = 523.

Full grid reference for point **X** = 877523.

Conditions underfoot can vary considerably with terrain and weather conditions. Good quality walking boots are a virtual necessity, as is waterproof clothing.

I wish you as much pleasure and satisfaction in following these walks as I derived from researching and compiling them.

Ted Parkes
Yeaveley
May 1993

FOLLOW THE COUNTRY CODE

Enjoy the countryside and respect its life and work.

Guard against all risks of fire.

Fasten all gates.

Keep your dogs under close control.

Keep to public paths across farmland.

Use gates and stiles to cross fences, hedges and walls.

Leave livestock, crops and machinery alone.

Take your litter home.

Protect wild life, plants and trees.

Take special care on country roads.

Make no unnecessary noise.

THE WALKS

Walk No.	Route/Distance	Page No.
1	Ilam - Musden Grange - Calton - Slade House - Soles Hollow - Beeston Tor - Wall Ditch - Castern - Ilam. (9½ miles)	1
2	Ilam - Air Cottage - Milldale - Alstonefield - Wetton - Beeston Tor - Throwley - Ilam. (10½ miles)	5
3	Ilam - Coldwall Bridge - Okeover - Blore - Musden Low - Dog Lane Farm - Ilam. (8½ miles)	10
4	Ilam - Dovedale - Moor Barn - Bostern Grange - Milldale - Stanshope - Wall Ditch - Castern - Bunster - Ilam. (10 miles)	14
5	Middle Mayfield - Lord's Piece - Cuckoo Cliff - Stanton - Weaver Hill - Wootton - Ellastone - Middle Mayfield. (10 miles)	17
6	Dimmings Dale - Stoney Dale - Hawksmoor Reserve - East Wall Farm - Ross Bridge - Whiston - Rock Cottage - Cotton Bank Farm - Oldsclough - Old Star - Farley - Dimmings Dale. (10 miles)	22
7	Milldale - Hall Dale - Damgate - Bincliffe - Wetton - Gateham Farm - Alstonefield - Milldale. (10 miles)	26
8	Alstonefield - Wetton - (Thor's Cave) Manifold Trail - Pepper's Inn - Ecton Hill - Apes Tor - Archford Moor Farm - Field House Farm - Narrow Dale - Alstonefield. (9 miles)	30
9	Alstonefield - Narrow Dale - Hartington - Heathcote - Biggin - Biggin Dale - Peasland Rocks - Alstonefield. (9 miles)	35

THE WALKS (Continued)

Walk No.	Route/Distance		Page No.
10	Monyash - Flagg - Chelmorton - Taddington - Sheldon - Monyash.		
		(11 miles)	38
11	Monyash - Sheldon - Over Haddon - Lathkill Dale - Monyash.		
		(10 miles)	44
12	Monyash - Sheldon - Over Haddon - Alport - Lathkill Dale - Monyash.		
		(13 miles)	49
13	Alport - Coal Pit Lane - Youlgreave - Bradford Dale - Elton - Harthill Moor - Alport.		
		(9 miles)	52
14	Alport - Over Haddon - Lathkill Lodge - Meadow Place Grange - Bradford Dale - Rock Farm - Anthony Hill - Mawstone Farm - Alport.		
		(9 miles)	57
15	Hartington - Pilsbury Castle - Crowdecote - Longnor - Lower Boothlow - Hill End - Sheen - Hartington.		
		(9½ miles)	62
16	Longnor - Earl Sterndale - Dowel Dale - Washgate - Hollinsclough - Hardings Booth - Longnor.		
		(9½ miles)	67
17	Parwich - Upper Moor Farm - Cobblers Nook Lane - Green Lane - High Peak Trail - Gallowlow Lane - Roystone Grange - Parwich.		
		(9 miles)	70
18	Tissington - Spend Lane - Bostern Grange - Alsop-En-Le-Dale - Parwich - Lea Hall - Tissington.		
		(10 miles)	74

THE WALKS (Continued)

Walk No.	Route/Distance		Page No.
19	Hollinsclough - Hollinsclough Moor - Thick Withins - Wickenlow - Blackbank - Wilson Knowl - Wildstone Rock - Far Brook - Three Shire Heads - Ready Leech Green - Axe Edge End - Nether Colshaw - Washgate - Hollinsclough.	(10 miles)	78
20	Errwood Reservoir - Errwood Hall Ruins - Shining Tor - Pym Chair - Windgather Rocks - Overton Hall Farm - Fernilee Reservoir - Errwood Reservoir	(9 miles)	83
21	Wetton Mill - Butterton - Onecote - Ford - Felthouse - Grindon - Ossom's Hill - Wetton Mill.	(9 miles)	87
22	Wetton Mill - Sugar Loaf - Ecton - Warslow - Upper Elkstone - Butterton - Wetton Mill.	(9 miles)	91
23	Rushton Spencer - Weathercock Farm - Hollinhall - Danebridge - Wincle Grange - Nettlebeds - Nabbs Hill - Wincle Minn - Barleighford Bridge - Rushton Spencer.	(10 miles)	95
24	Bearstone Rock (Roach End) - Forest Wood - Gradbach YHA - Three Shire Heads - Wildboarclough - Goosetree - Back Forest Ridge - Bearstone Rock.	(10½ miles)	99
25	Gradbach - Bennettsich - Parks - Wildboarclough - Hammerton Knowl - Wild Boar Inn - Hammerton Farm - Danebridge - Gradbach.	(9½ miles)	103
26	Ashford - Monsal Head - Upperdale - Water-cum-Jolly Dale - Miller's Dale - Brushfield - Great Shacklow Wood - Ashford.	(9½ miles)	107

THE WALKS (Continued)

Walk No.	Route/Distance	Page No.
27	Winster Top - Limestone Way - Brightgate - Wensley - Watt's Shaft - Stanton Moor - Birchover - Winster Top. (9 miles)	111
28	Baslow - Baslow Edge - Curbar Edge - Froggart Edge - Haywood - Grindleford - Froggart - Calver - Curbar - Baslow. (10 miles)	117
29	Hathersage - North Lees - Green's House - Stanage Edge - Higger Tor - Carl Wark - Mitchell Fields - Hathersage. (8 miles)	121
30	Eyam - Foolow - Abney Moor - Offerton Hall - Offerton Moor - Abney - Stoke Ford - Sir William Hill - Eyam. (11 miles)	125
31	Eyam - Stoney Middleton - Froggart - Grindleford - Leadmill Bridge- Hazelford Hall - Stoke Ford - Mompesson's Well - Eyam. (10 miles)	130
32	Foolow - Silly Dale - Grindlow - Great Hucklow - Little Hucklow - Bradwell - Abney - Stoke Ford - Bretton - Foolow. (10 miles)	134
33	Castleton - Lose Hill - Hollins Cross - Mam Tor - Rushup Edge - Barber Booth - Hollins Cross - Castleton. (11 miles)	138
34	Castleton - Lose Hill Hall - Lose Hill Farm - Townhead - Bagshaw Bridge - Win Hill Pike - Aston - Hope - Castleton. (10 miles)	143
35	Monsal Trail - Chee Dale - Mosley Farm - Tunstead - Hargatewall - Peter's Dale - Wormhill - Monsal Trail. (9 miles)	147

Walk 1	Ilam - Musden Grange - Calton - Slade House - Soles Hollow - Beeston Tor - Wall Ditch - Castern - Ilam.
	(9½ miles)
Description	A superbly scenic walk around the Hamps and Manifold Valley area and including the attractive village of Calton.
Map	OS Map Outdoor Leisure No. 24, scale 1:25000.
Start	Ilam village (roadside parking), ref. 134508.

Route

1. Go left through gate at bottom of Hall drive on the path past the church[1] to the Hall[2], turn left across the front and descend to the riverside path - Paradise Walk[3].

2. Follow the path upstream, past the 'Boil Holes'[4], cross stile/gate and footbridge across River Manifold.

3. Go half right through two stiles, along two more stiled fields, turn left alongside wall of third, cross Musden Grange[5] drive via a gate, to a footpath sign.

4. Climb alongside the boundary wall as directed, at the wall end ignore the track going left, keep climbing alongside the wall and trees, cross a broken wall to a signpost for Calton at a footpath junction.

5. Continue as indicated, through two stiles, pass in front of barn to second Calton sign, follow boundary wall up hill and near top turn left to a stile.

   Look back for superb view across a section of the Manifold Valley with half right the 350 million years old limestone reef hills of Bunster and Thorpe Cloud.

6. Cross the stile, descend the field, on to a lane, keep ahead up the lane, and round the bend to cross a facing stile.

7. Go half right on a nearly straight line, across two stiles, through a gate near farm buildings and two more stiles to reach a road.

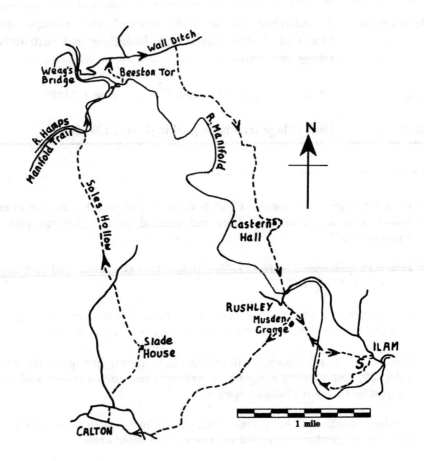

8. Turn right, straight over at the crossroads and so into Calton; opposite the telephone box turn right on a track past the seventeenth century Post Office to a road.

9. Go right, left as signed *Throwley and Ilam*, right again at green footpath sign along rough road to Slade House.

10. Leave on track left, cross Calton - Throwley road by signpost, continuing straight ahead passing close left to a small reservoir, follow boundary walls down a little valley, join a hollow way (Soles Hollow), first grassy then rocky after crossing a stile, ending at the Manifold Trail[6].

11. Go right along the trail, leaving it near Beeston Tor, a favourite rock face with climbers, cross a bridge at the confluence of rivers Hamps and Manifold, go left through a small gate by footpath sign and cross the river by stepping stones to stile opposite.

    NB Not practical during winter months when river has a good flow but most of the year the bed is dry or has little water.

    A diversion is to follow the trail to Weag's Bridge, go up the road over the bridge to rejoin the route at a cattle grid.

12. Go forward from the stile, turn left along a track, at its end go left side of wall to join the Wetton road at a cattle grid.

13. Turn right, along Wall Ditch (packhorse route, Grindon to Alstonefield) for approximately 600 yards, cross stile on right and one opposite across narrow field, contour along hillside to cross a third (to right of water trough), on to a clear path rising to the rim of the Manifold Valley with excellent views across and down the valley.

14. Follow path right through to end of boundary wall, cross stile, turn left to single standing stone (old way marker?) then right on a ridge path down the field to join a stiled/gated track through to Castern Hall, (late eighteenth century).

15. Leave by the Hall drive, after first 'loop' cross grass and stile (by tree), go left round the bank, rejoin the drive for a few yards, leave it half right on field path, cross stile hidden by trees then on to Rushley Bridge.

16. Cross the bridge, angle left to wall stile, keep ahead across the field to rejoin the outward route back to Paradise Walk and Ilam.

17. For an alternative way back from the footbridge take the track left of the stile/gate, half way up go left across the ridge and furrows (medieval farming method) of the Park to join a track through to the village, opposite school.

Background Information

(1) Ilam Church

Blocked door and wall on south side is probably Saxon. Tower base is thirteenth century.

South Chapel built 1618 by Meverell of Throwley Hall, Hurt of Castern and Port of Ilam. Their initials are over the doors. Contains tomb and shrine of St. Bertram, tomb cover of ninth century, shrine 1386.

Font Saxon or Norman.

Two ancient crosses in churchyard, taller one c.900, other c.1000.

(2) Ilam Hall

Built 1826-28 by Jesse Watts-Russell replacing earlier one by John Port (1546).

National Trust property since 1934.

(3) Paradise Walk

So called because of its beautiful setting lined with lime and beech trees.

(4) Boil Holes

Here the Rivers Hamps and Manifold emerge from their subterranean meanderings.

(5) Musden Grange (Musedene in Domesday Book)

Once a monastic sheep farm house in the possession of Burton Abbey. Present building started in sixteenth century.

(6) Manifold Trail

Track bed of the defunct Leek and Manifold Light Railway, opened in 1904 to serve hillside villages; closed in 1934 - economically unviable.

Walk 2	**Ilam - Air Cottage - Milldale - Alstonefield - Wetton - Beeston Tor - Throwley - Ilam.**
	(10½ miles)
Description	**A mainly high-level walk with superb views, excursions into Dove and Manifold Valleys, plus four villages.**
Map	**OS Map Outdoor Leisure No. 24, scale 1:25000.**
Start	**Ilam village (roadside parking), ref. 134508.**

Route

1. Leave the village left of the monument (1840) to Jesse Watts-Russell's wife, go through small gate by fingerpost, up the bank in front, follow track contouring left round base of Bunster Hill.

2. Follow the distinct path past St. Bertram's Well[1], continue uphill (ignore stile left) alongside boundary wall, cross corner stile, set back left by thorn tree.

3. Turn up the field, go through gate in top wall (near barn), turn left along path, go right along drive to Air Cottage[2], either take stiled path right, round the house or concession path through the yard.

4. Cross ladder stile ahead right into Dovedale Wood, follow distinct path first along the edge of the wood then on a winding descent to the bank of the river in Dovedale.

5. Follow the river upstream (dippers are not uncommon along here), cross a stile, pass Dove Hole caves right, cross another stile, follow path rising along hillside through edge of a wood ending with short descent from Achas Bank into Milldale[3] adjacent to toilets and Viator's Bridge[4].

6. Go right at the little cottage shop, up Millway Lane (packhorse way), which steadily ascends to Alstonefield[5] Church and Manor House (built 1587, year before Armada) then village green with its coaching inn, The George.

7. Bear left, passing Old Post Office tea room and current Post Office and shop, go straight across at road junction on track past Memorial Hall.

8. Cross stile at track end, another one opposite, by a tree, go part right through two more stiles to lane.

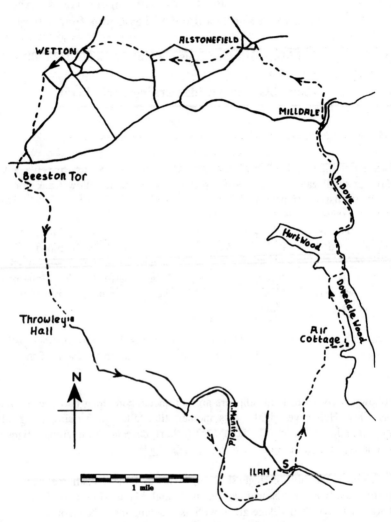

9. Go straight across, again on clear path, over several stiles (ignore one right at path junction), waymarked through a paddock to the lane again.

10. Ignore stile opposite, turn right to corner, go left through stile on to green lane, leave it via stile left opposite large tree.

11. Cross ladder stile seen ahead, carry on up the field on slight left curve, cross stile near right corner, one ahead at external corner then cross field on diagonal to reach road via stile/gate.

12. Walk up the road into Wetton[6], turn right opposite the Old Royal Oak pub, left at the corner (Manor House Farm to right is seventeenth century), past little café to road junction.

13. Opposite and adjacent to Grindon sign are a footpath sign and stile at cottage garden corner. Cross the stile, lawn, stile and stile near gate, continue up the concrete track and through stile by left gate of two.

14. Keep ahead across two more stiles, then diagonally left to stile, footpath sign and lane (to Weag's Bridge).

15. Turn right, just round the bend go right over stile, descend field to rejoin lane at cattle grid, cross this then immediately left over stile to follow wall to its end.

16. Go left down a track, right at the end, cross stile, ford river on to a track, via a small gate, near the confluence of rivers Hamps and Manifold. The rock face left is Beeston Tor[7], popular with climbers.

17. Follow the track, signed for Throwley, to its end, cross stile and ascend field, across 1000 year old 'strip lynchets' (cultivation terraces), on a line left of main body of trees to stile left of gateway.

18. Descend field to left corner of spinney, cross stile, follow path through to Throwley Hall farmyard, turn right, pass through gate, follow road (public thoroughfare) winding down the valley to Rushley. The ruins left are of the Hall built 1603 by Samson Meverell, present Hall is early nineteenth century.

19. Cross open field left of Rushley Farm, go through stile, keep straight ahead on distinct path over fields to cross footbridge over River Manifold to Paradise Walk.

20. Return to Ilam[8] village as Walk 1.

Background Information

(1) St. Bertram (Bertilin)

Son of ninth century King of Mercia. Became hermit after wife and child killed by wolves. Renounced heritage for meditation and prayer; converted many pagans to Christianity.

In Middle Ages his shrine was scene of apparently miraculous cures.

(2) Air Cottage

Built here, and so called, by a couple (so the story goes) to ensure an abundance of fresh air to ease suffering of their very asthmatic daughter.

(3) Milldale

As the name implies there was once a mill here but little evidence remains other than the mill stream.

(4) Viator's Bridge

A centuries-old packhorse bridge; the parapets then would be lower than now to give clearance for the panniers.

In 1676, Charles Cotton of Beresford Hall, wrote an addendum to the 5th edition of his great friend, Izaak Walton's book *The Compleat Angler*.

He wrote of a fictitious interlude in which Piscator (Cotton) was taking Viator (a traveller from Essex) across the bridge whereupon Viator asked, "Do you travel in wheel barrows in this country? - the bridge is not two fingers broad." Hence the name Viator's Bridge.

(5) Alstonefield (Ænestanefelt in Domesday Book)

An important medieval market town (charter 1308) and a crossing point of several packhorse ways.

Once the centre of a large parish of 24,000 acres including Warslow, Elkstones, Quarnford and Longnor (then an isolated chapelry) with a total population of 5,000.

Church

> Third on site. First dated AD 892, second Norman, present one fourteenth/fifteenth century but much altered in 1590. Near the font are Saxon artefacts including stone coffin and eight-sided font.

(6) Wetton (not in Domesday book)

> Saxon origin but earlier settlement - Romano-British - found on edge of present village at Borough Fields.

(7) Beeston Tor

> In cave at the foot were found a hoard of ninth century Saxon coins and flint evidence of earlier occupation.

(8) Ilam   See Walk 1.

Walk 3	**Ilam - Coldwall Bridge - Okeover - Blore - Musden Low - Dog Lane Farm - Ilam.**
	(8½ miles)
Description	**A walk of contrasts between river side meadows, an ancient family estate and limestone hills.**
Map	**OS Map Outdoor Leisure No. 24, scale 1:25000, also Pathfinder Series SK04/14, scale 1:25000.**
Start	**Ilam village (roadside parking), ref. 134508.**

Route

1. Cross the stile at far left corner of river bridge on to the path alongside the River Manifold, follow to the confluence of rivers Dove and Manifold near Fishpond Wood; continue along the waymarked path, which now leaves the riverside, through to Coldwall Bridge[1], a large stone structure looking somewhat out of place at the bottom of a field.

2. Turn right at far end of bridge, down a farm track, cross a stile, go left on a path to right of farm buildings continuing alongside the river to where it loops right to cross a weir.

3. Leave the river, go straight ahead across a field to rejoin the riverside through to Okeover Bridge.

4. Cross the bridge, turn left along the road through Okeover Park, leaving at the Hall[2] drive, ascend the hillside, between trees, pass a gamekeeper's derelict house, cross a stile at a wood corner.

5. Keep straight ahead to a field corner, turn left to join a walled track, leading to Martin Hill farm, go right by side of old barn (not as shown on OS map) continue ahead along field boundaries to join another walled track through to Woodhouses.

6. Follow the single track lane up to Blore's[3] interesting little church, just before churchyard turn between stone pillars, go through gateway ahead then over stile/gate, follow right wall to its corner, continue straight ahead along a little

10

valley and two gated fields to reach the eighteenth century Cheadle to Thorpe
turnpike road via a stile at end of third field.

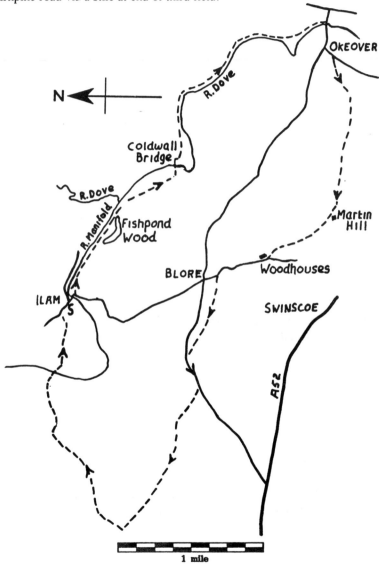

1 mile

7. Approximately 200 yards to left, turn right along an overgrown track between a wall and fence, cross a gate, follow left boundary which swings left up the hillside, leaving it near the top to go right to a stile and blocked gateway in facing wall.

8. Cross over, swing right (ignore stile in facing wall) past the rocky outcrop, tumulus and disused lime kiln, to join and follow left boundary wall, cross double stile at its end.

9. On the same path line, cross gate ahead, two fields and two more gates on to narrow lane at Doglane Farm.

    The gates may have to be climbed - farmer does not actively encourage walkers.

10. Cross stile on right, ascend field alongside boundary, cross stile at the top with superb view across Manifold Valley, follow left wall down the field to corner signpost.

11. Go left as directed, pass in front of barn to corner stile, cross field and stile ahead to another sign at footpath junction.

12. Turn right (Ilam), in second field go half left to cross track from Musden Grange, swing left on clear path steeply descending fields to cross footbridge onto Paradise Walk[4].

13. Go right along the walk, over the Boil Holes[5], left up to Ilam Hall[6] and return to the village via the Church[7] path.

Background Information

(1) Coldwall Bridge

Built in 1760's to carry the Cheadle to Thorpe turnpike road connecting with the Derby to Manchester road at Spend Lane.

(2) Okeover Hall (Acoure in Domesday Book)

Estate held by the Okeover family in direct male descent for over 800 years until 1955 when last male Haughton-Okeover died.

Nephew Sir Ian Walker of Osmaston Manor added Okeover to his name and moved in.

Hall timbered and moated prior to 1745, the year Leake Okeover started rebuilding; east range buildings and magnificent stable block are from this period.

Church - aisleless. Decorated style with perpendicular tower (fourteenth to sixteenth centuries).

(3) Blore Church

'Blore' derives from '*blora*'- 'a windy place'. Mentioned in Domesday Book and eleventh century records of Burton Abbey. Church is fourteenth/fifteenth centuries. Nave has original fifteenth century benches, box pews are seventeenth century.

North chapel contains magnificent alabaster monument (c.1640) to William Basset whose family were Lords of the Manor for 500 years - arrived with William the Conqueror.

(4) Paradise Walk	See Walk 1.
(5) Boil Holes	See Walk 1.
(6) Ilam Hall	See Walk 1.
(7) Ilam Church	See Walk 1.

13

Walk 4	Ilam - Dovedale - Moor Barn - Bostern Grange - Milldale - Stanshope - Wall Ditch - Castern - Bunster - Ilam.
	(10 miles)
Description	Mainly a high level walk with extensive views and including an introduction to Dovedale.
Map	OS Map Outdoor Leisure No. 24, scale 1:25000.
Start	Roadside in Ilam[1] Village, ref. 134508.

Route

1. Go left of the large monument (1840) in memory of Jesse Watts-Russel's wife, to a footpath sign and small gate, go right on clear stiled field path through to Dovedale car park, with mobile refreshment van and public toilets.

2. Turn left at the car park, cross footbridge and follow river upstream past the Stepping Stones and up the stepped path to Lovers Leap.

3. Take the path right through the trees then follow a shallow depression bearing first right then left on a steep ascent, when near the top go left to signpost and stile.

4. Cross over to follow boundary wall on to Moor Barn drive, at its end angle left to reach a three-way signpost.

5. Cross the stile, go through gateway left then half right on a waymarked path to Bostern Grange, passing a good example of a lime kiln near to a spinney on the left.

6. Pass through the farmyard and straight ahead across three fields then turn left as directed on a straight path, later descending steeply on a zig-zag near its end into Milldale via Viator's Bridge[2].

   An excellent break spot with small shop providing refreshments; also public toilets here.

7. Walk away from the river, up Hope Dale for about 150 yards to a signpost near a cottage, follow the stony path up the hillside, then straight ahead along field boundaries on to a track descending to Stanshope.

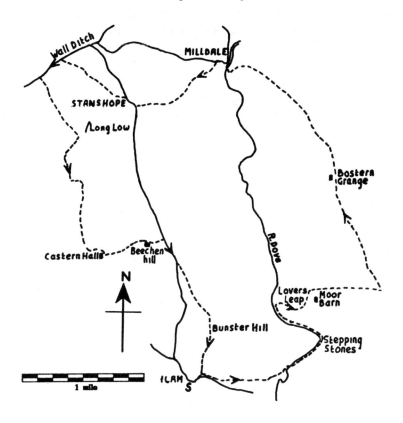

8. Turn right to follow the road past Grange Farm to a signpost and stile, cross the field diagonally to another stile, then follow left boundary across three more stiles, keep straight ahead across the dip, cross stile left of gate.

9. Go right to cross stile left of gate, take a line on left end of trees ahead, cross wall stile and one beyond trees on to Wall Ditch, a little used single track lane originally a packhorse way on the route from Grindon via Weag's Bridge to Alstonefield.

10. Turn left up the lane, left at the crossroads to reach a very tall three-way signpost. Ahead and left is a long mound surmounted by a wall - this is Long Low[3].

11. Take path right, signed Castern, which passes shafts (capped) and spoil heaps of the disused Highfield lead mine, gradually being reclaimed by Nature, cross stile on to path running along the rim of a section of the Manifold Valley. Fine views along and over the valley.

12. Turn left to wall end, left again to single standing stone (old waymarker?) then right along a ridge path on to a stiled/gated track through to Castern Hall, late eighteenth century.

13. From the side of the Hall go left to signpost (Ilam Moor), carry on up the field on a slightly right bearing to a stile in facing wall some 20 yards from right corner, continue on similar line to cross stile in right wall.

14. The path heads towards Beechenhill Farm, left round the buildings, down the drive to the Ilam-Stanshope road.

15. Go down the road on to Air Cottage drive, leave immediately by stile on right, pass close to trees seen ahead, then follow clear path line descending steeply to the flank of Bunster Hill, turn right along path past St Bertram's Well[4], to the little roadside gate where the walk effectively started.

Background Information

(1) Ilam	See Walk 1.
(2) Viator's Bridge	See Walk 2.
(3) Long Low	See Walk 7.
(4) St Bertram's Well	See Walk 2.

Walk 5	Middle Mayfield - Lord's Piece - Cuckoo Cliff - Stanton - Weaver Hill - Wootton - Ellastone - Middle Mayfield.
	(10 miles)
Description	An attractive walk in a quiet area just outside the White Peak. Good long range views.
Map	OS Map Pathfinder 810 Sheet SK04/14, scale 1:25000.
Start	Roadside in Middle Mayfield near Old Hall Farm, ref. 147448.

Route

1. Go through stile at bottom of Hollow Lane, swing up field along right boundary, continue to the top to meet a track and a facing stile.

2. Turn right, follow through to Stanton road, cross stile at left corner of Lord's Piece drive, follow left boundary through gate and stile beyond.

3. Go half right, cross stile by gate, follow right boundary, cross fence and stile, continue along the boundary and round the corner, cross another stile.

4. Keep ahead before turning up the field, pass through gate to wall stile on right, turn half left, go through gateway, pass right of Newhouse Farm on to drive.

5. Cross cattle grid, short of second one go through gate ahead in field on right, turn half right on a straight line across three stiles, turn right to cross a fourth with Leasow Farm house ahead right.

6. Go left round rough patch, cross stile, keep straight ahead across Ellis Hill to a fence, descend alongside, cross stile on to steps down into the pleasant little valley under Cuckoo Cliff.

7. Continue across the stream and stile at top of field, follow right boundary to join Flather Lane through to Stanton[1].

8. Turn right along the road, keep left at junctions, to the church of 1847, cross stile right, follow path which crosses little stream then rises to steps and stile right of house.

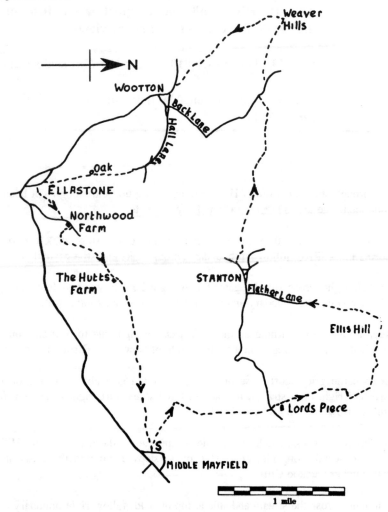

9. Two paths meet here, ignore clear one sraight ahead, take diagonal line to stile near corner then ahead to gate in next field.

10. Cross the farm track, keep ahead with wall on right, cross two stiles to a little brook, follow upstream to fenced fish pond.

11. Go through gate at far end of fence, cross stream, go up field, pass through gate and another further on and right, continue up the field to a third gate and Back Lane.

    A short way left down the lane are humps and hollows of disused Raddle Pits[2].

12. Turn right, follow left boundary to a stile, cross over and follow first right boundary, then left across two fields, cross stile, go right along boundary to short of field corner.

13. Turn left at 90º to a wall outer corner, follow wall down slope, cross stile (the one in the wall is for concession path to trig point) then leave the wall to contour round the hill, gradually gaining height, before descending to cross stile in right wall.

14. Go left, cross stile in far wall, cross field to far right corner, follow track on to Gidacre Lane (track) through to road at Wootton.

15. Follow road left, keep straight ahead at the bend into Wootton, go left at the fork, past Back Lane on to Hall Lane, continue to its end at Wootton Hall Farm.

16. Cross stile left at signpost, turn right alongside boundary, on a straight line cross stile and a stream to a single oak tree.

17. Continue on a slightly left bearing, descend to cross fence stile and footbridge at far side of field, ascend field to solitary house where refreshments are obtainable.

18. Leave by the drive, follow lane left and ascend steps into Ellastone Churchyard[3], take path left, go through kissing gate, bear left to cross a stile on to a clear path line past a house and across fields to a narrow lane.

19. Turn left to far end of Northwood Farm buildings, cross stile then footbridge at field bottom, turn left along boundary, cross stile, continue on a slight arc right to The Hutts Farm.

19

20. Go straight ahead through the yard on to the drive, where this turns left leave through a gate, follow boundary across two stiled fields (ignore stile on left).

21. In third field go half right to wall corner, straight ahead to one opposite, follow boundary across two stiles.

22. Cross next field on diagonal line, through gate turn left to cross Dyden Farm drive, go through gate then half right to cross stile on to track.

23. Turn left past field boundary, take diagonal line across two fields, cross stile in corner of second.

24. Continue alongside rough grassy area, pass through a clump of holly to a stile ahead - *do not cross*. Turn right on a wide path through trees and scrub, pass through kissing gate at the end, cross stile on to Hollow Lane, follow path back to Middle Mayfield[4].

Background Information

(1) Stanton (Stantone in Domesday Book)

Typical hilltop village of stone built houses; is the birthplace of Gilbert Sheldon (1598-1677), an Archbishop of Canterbury.

(2) Raddle Pits

'Raddle' is a corruption of 'reddle' - red ochre, a clayey oxide of iron used for pigments.

(3) Ellastone (Edelachestone or Elachestone, both in Domesday Book)

Old hall by roadside in middle of village is late seventeenth century.

The village is Hayslope of George Eliot's *Adam Bede*. Her father, Robert Evans, spent his early life here as a carpenter.

Church is largely late sixteenth century, tower dated 1586.

(4) Middle Mayfield (Medevelde in Domesday Book)

Along with Upper and Church Mayfield, makes up the sprawling community known collectively as Mayfield.

Hall - late Georgian with grand stables and domed stone cupola (projecting dome).

Old Hall - gabled house of early seventeenth century.

Walk 6	Dimmings Dale - Stoney Dale - Hawksmoor Reserve - East Wall Farm - Ross Bridge - Whiston - Rock Cottage - Cotton Bank Farm - Oldsclough - Old Star - Farley - Dimmings Dale.
	(10 miles)
Description	Delightful Dimmings Dale, riverside meadows, a deer park together with excellent views make this a very attractive walk.
Map	OS Map Pathfinder 810 sheet, SK04/14, scale 1:25000.
Start	Rambler's Retreat, Dimmings Dale, ref. 063433.

Route

1. Dimmings Dale with its trees, rhododendrons, brook and fishponds was created by the Earl of Shrewsbury in the nineteenth century.

   Follow the wide path (carriageway) past the ruins of the lead smelting mill, for aproximately ¾ mile, cross wide path between two fishponds, ascend path through the trees, cross stile and continue ahead to the YHA.

2. Follow the rough track left to Stoney Dale, turn right down the lane to signpost left, ascend path through the wood to the road above Oakamoor, cross left to Hawksmoor Nature Reserve.

3. Follow the track down through the Reserve to East Wall Farm, go as waymarked round the farm past the attractive lake with large mixed population of water fowl, continue on the distinct path through the riverside meadows of the Churnet to the far side of a marshy field (spiky, tufty grass).

4. Go slightly right along a path, cross a small footbridge followed by the new Ross Bridge over the Churnet and one over the defunct Churnet Valley Railway.

5. The way ahead is Ross Lane, an old track between hedges, augmented these days by another path up the open field. At the top follow the metalled lane nearly to the end of the hollow section, go right, up the bank, cross stile adjacent to

electricity pole, follow path across two fields, cross stile at house garden, follow path through to cul-de-sac and road ahead.

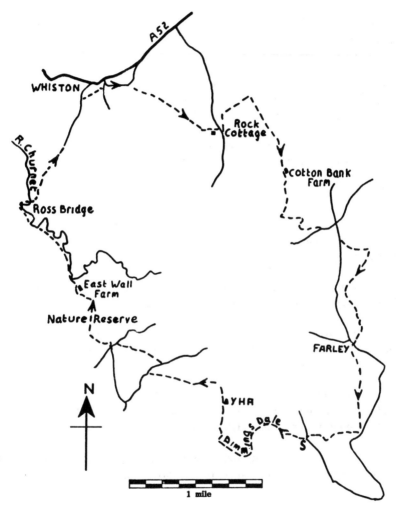

6. Turn left (Post Office and shop along here), right up Black Lane to footpath sign at Whiston Golf Course, follow wide grassy path across course in front of teeing grounds (take care), past a very large boulder right, to a stile.

7. The path ahead is clearly stiled across fields, through a small wood, across a small field to the aptly named Rock Cottage and a road.

8. Cross right to a footpath sign, follow overgrown walled track to field corner stile, ascend fields alongside wall, cross stile and descend to Bridle Path (Staffordshire Moorlands Walk).

9. Turn right, follow path to just beyond Cotton Bank Farm, section ahead is private, go right on path through trees, left at the top as waymarked, left again (*not right as waymarked*) down to path left earlier.

10. Cross the stile and one ahead at the wood, descend steps into Oldsclough, an attractive wooded valley with brook, cross footbridge, follow path all the way up the hillside to a road.

11. Turn left (Old Star Inn ahead) to crossroads, go right (Beelow Lane) to opening on left (opposite farm drive) leading to the deer park of Sir Anthony Bamford (head of JCB Manufacturers). Several herds of deer will be seen whilst passing through the park.

12. Go through metal kissing gate/stile, through gate on right, follow fence line over the hill, pass through gate at barn corner on to track.

13. Turn right, pass through two gates, go slightly right across slope to cross gate/stile, follow hillside path, cross stile at end, continue past cottages to road through Farley.

14. Cross stiles opposite into a large field, JCB Equestrian Centre to right, cross field diagonally left on to private drive. The large white building seen from the field is the nineteenth century Hall, home of Sir Anthony Bamford.

15. Pass through the gate opposite and one at field bottom, take a line through middle of trees, across two stiles on to private drive with old lodge house; tower structure held water tank.

    En route are fine views across to Alton Towers[1] and Castle[2] left, and Churnet Valley woods right.

16. Cross the drive, go right on path (Barbary Gutter) descending through trees, cross defunct railway bridge and Lord's Bridge over River Churnet, go through gate back to Rambler's Retreat[3].

Background Information

(1) Alton Towers

Gardens and house started 1814 by fifteenth Earl of Shrewsbury and continued after his death by sixteenth Earl. Became principal 'seat' in 1831. Deteriorated after seventeenth Earl died in 1856 when Shrewsburys moved to Ingestre Hall.

Sold in 1924 and developed, intensively in last decade, to become internationally known theme park.

(2) Castle

Rhineland style, built 1847-52 by sixteenth Earl, close to site of original medieval castle.

(3) Rambler's Retreat

Originally a lodge house at the beginning of Earl's (Shrewsbury) Way through Dimmings Dale. Now very popular with both walkers and motorists; good reputation for refreshments.

Walk 7	Milldale - Hall Dale - Damgate - Bincliffe - Wetton - Gateham Farm - Alstonefield - Milldale.
	(10 miles)
Description	**Another walk in that beautifully scenic area around the Dove and Manifold Valleys.**
Map	**OS Map Outdoor Leisure No. 24, scale 1:25000.**
Start	**Public car park above Milldale in Hopedale, ref. 138547.**

Route

1. Walk down the road to the River Dove with ancient packhorse bridge (Viator's[1]), take the path right of toilets, turn left at the top, follow distinct path along hillside gradually dropping across stiled fields to the riverside.

2. Continue alongside the river (look out for dippers), past Dove Holes caves to a grassy clearing just beyond where path passes close to rock face.

3. Turn right on path steadily ascending Hall Dale, short of fourth stile cross stile left, follow boundary wall to a walled track. Left is a disused lime kiln shielded by trees.

4. Follow the track to just beyond a barn, cross field corner stile, go on diagonal across field to stile and road.

5. Cross stile opposite right, and another diagonally across the field, turn right, go through gate, keep straight ahead following right boundary across several fields to a very tall three-way signpost.

   When nearing the signpost look right to see a 220 yard long mound surmounted by a wall; this is Long Low[2].

6. Follow path left, signed Castern, past the disused Highfield lead mine, cross stile on to footpath traversing edge of Manifold Valley between Beeston Tor and Ilam. Excellent viewpoint.

7. Turn right, follow path through to its end where it descends to cross small field on to narrow lane (Wall Ditch).

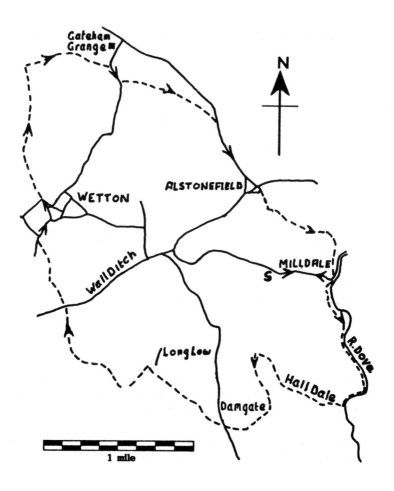

8. Follow footpath opposite, up the field, cross wall stile, descend to cross stile in right corner, turn right along the road into Wetton[3], past the toilets to road junction.

9. Go left up the road, past the The Old Royal Oak pub to sharp left bend, with seventeenth century Manor House Farm on right, leave road and continue ahead up rough track signed Back of Ecton, past reservoir, cross stile on to Wetton Hill.

10. Carry on straight ahead before descending across the contours to cross narrow field via two stiles, continue down to wall corner.

11. Leave wall, maintain a fairly constant height, contour round to join a path on far side of hill, follow this to a wall stile on left near gate, cross field beyond and stile near gate on to road with Gateham Grange[4] to left.

12. Turn right then first left along the drive and through the yard of Gateham Farm, cross stile in facing wall and another straight across the field, on to a narrow lane.

13. Go through stile opposite (footpath signpost misleadingly points right), turn half left, cross wall stile, adjacent to large hedge gap, go right alongside the wall across two stiles, the path continues on the same line across three fields then on a slight right curve to join the Alstonefield road at a footpath sign.

14. Turn right for Alstonefield[5], left at the fork, toilets are along here, left at junction then right to far left corner of village green.

    The seventeenth century George Inn is at side of green and round the corner are The Old Post Office Tea Rooms, current post office and shop.

15. Carry on towards the Church[6], with Manor House (1587) left and eighteenth century old vicarage right, continue down the old packhorse route, Millway Lane, to Milldale, turn right for car park.

    NB An alternative route is via field path - distinct line from signpost below churchyard. Descends steeply near its end - requires good grip footwear.

Background Information

(1) Viator's Bridge   See Walk 2.

(2) Long Low

Two neolithic chambered tombs joined together by a long bank; northern one contained remains of 13 people plus flint knife and arrow heads.

(3) Wetton   See Walk 2.

(4) Gateham Grange

Once medieval monastic farm of Combermere Abbey, Cheshire.

(5) Alstonefield   See Walk 2.

   (6) Church   See Walk 2.

Walk 8	Alstonefield - Wetton - (Thor's Cave) Manifold Trail - Pepper's Inn - Ecton Hill - Apes Tor - Archford Moor Farm - Field House Farm - Narrow Dale - Alstonefield.
	(9 miles)
Description	A walk of contrasts between the magnificent and popular Manifold Valley and quieter less used paths back to Alstonefield; many fine views.
Map	OS Map Outdoor Leisure No. 24, scale 1:25000.
Start	Public car park in Alstonefield, ref. 131556.

Route

1. Turn left from the car park, pass the road junction, go left at footpath signpost on a track then a field path along boundaries, left initially then right after a stile, to reach a narrow lane.

2. Follow this right to a bend with a house and a barn nearby, cross stile on to green lane, leave it via stile opposite large tree.

3. Cross ladder stile seen ahead, carry on up field on slight left curve, cross stile near right corner, one ahead at external corner, then diagonally cross field to a road via stile/gate.

4. Walk up the road into Wetton[1], turn right opposite The Old Royal Oak pub, follow the road past the seventeenth century Manor House Farm and a small café, to a junction.

5. Take the Wetton Mill road, cross stile on left just beyond the walled track, go up the middle of the field, cross a stile and keep ahead on what becomes a clear path descending steeply through trees to a footbridge over the River Manifold and the Manifold Trail, track bed of the long defunct valley railway.

   Part way down the path another goes left up to Thor's Cave[2] for those with energy to spare. The view from the cave is tremendous but, if wet underfoot, great care should be taken in getting down from the entrance and on the steep path descent back to the bottom of the basic route path.

6. Turn right along the trail to where the road from Wetton joins it, leave the trail here, cross the stile ahead (National Trust sign on right) into a delightful little valley (normally dry, but in wet weather can resemble a river), cross stile at the top on to access road adjacent to Pepper's Inn[3].

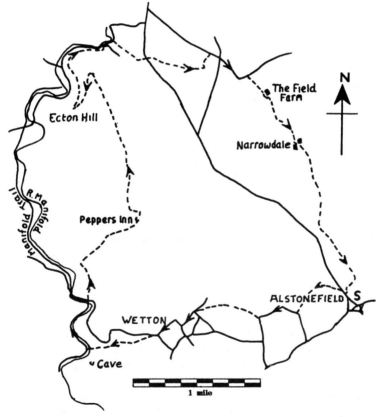

7. Follow road up and along the hillside to a fork, go left then shortly right through a gate on to a grassy path ending at the ruins of the Waterbank Mine, a major one of the 50-70 disused lead and copper mines (majority were lead) on the hill.

8. Continue through the ruins, cross stile ahead (ignore one left), bear slightly right to reach a wall corner and stile. About ten paces forward from the corner, an examination of the wall will reveal excellent examples of limestone rich in identifiable fossils. Follow the line of the wall sraight through to a stone building soon seen ahead; this is all that is left of the Ecton Hill Copper Mine[4] engine house.

   En route there are several fenced but uncapped mine shafts.

9. Short of the stile swing left down the hillside through more ruins, take path right to an odd looking house with a green copper spire[5].

   Although plenty of evidence remains of major mining activities, many of the spoil heaps were used in the construction of the Leek and Manifold Light Railway[6] track, now the Manifold Trail.

10. Having crossed the stile at the end of the path, walk in front of the house, cross stile ahead by gate then veer left to follow a path[7] which contours around the hill (Apes Tor) to a stile on left by signpost at footpath junction, cross over and descend field to narrow road at East Ecton.

11. A short diversion here is worthwhile.

   Turn left at the junction to a large opening in the rock face with a large capped hole in the floor and, a few yards further on, a smaller opening at a lower level.

   Here the first sough (water drainage tunnel) for the Ecton Copper Mine was started in 1723 and a second level 200 ft. down was cut about 1764.

   Both were later used for bringing out ore and stone in boats, lifted from the lower level by horse power. Later still, the original sough was used to take water *into* the mine to operate the hydraulic pumping engine installed therein.

   Note, in the cave and a short way up the road, the exposed rock face clearly illustrating how, millions of years ago, earth's massive internal forces moved the initially horizontal 'bedding' planes to near vertical in places.

12. Return along the road, past the road junction, on to a farm drive at the bend

ahead, leave it at the curve and, on a straight line, cross the wall stile just ahead and three other stiled crossings, then turn left up the boundary to a road.

13. Cross the stile opposite and one beyond left end of wall ahead, follow direction of waymarker across a hedge stile to far corner of next field, go left on clearly stiled way past the farm, veer left to cross two more stiles then right to stile near gate and a road.

14. Turn right along the road, straight on at the crossroads, follow the lane round the bend then go right down the drive to Field House Farm.

15. Pass right of the buildings then left on to a track and down to a gate, cross stile on left, go half left to cross three more stiles on to a hedged track which passes a ruined stone house and ends at a narrow water course.

16. Keep straight on through a wall stile left of a pair of trees and up the bank on to Narrow Dale[8] Farm drive, turn left then right between the buildings on to an ascending field path alongside a wall.

17. At the top of the rise by a wall stile, veer right on to a wide grassy path along the hillside, cross the stile at the end, follow the wall to its end then straight ahead across a field to a walled track.

18. Cross over to the stile half right by the trees, turn left to cross another, go through wall gap on left, turn right to follow a straight line path alongside right boundary across several stiled fields to a farm track, turn right, left at the fork, left again at the Alstonefield[9] road with the car park a short way ahead.

Background Information

    (1) Wetton   See Walk 1.

    (2) Thor's Cave

        Probably formed as part of a very early river system when the valley floor was much higher than today.

        Excavation finds of flint arrowheads, bone combs, bronze ornaments, iron adzes and Roman period pottery indicate occupation of the cave over thousands of years.

(3) Pepper's Inn

Dated 1825, once a public house serving the miners of Ecton Hill; peppercorns were given away with each pint.

The upper floor was, at one time, used as a button factory.

(4) Ecton Hill Copper Mine

See Walk 22.

(5) House   See Walk 22.

(6) Leek and Manifold Light Railway

Built in 1904 for the purpose of serving the hilltop communities either side of the Manifold Valley; proved economically unviable and closed in 1934.

It ran from Waterhouses to Hulme End, where some of the buildings still remain.

(7) Path

This is the route by which water was transported, along a gritstone trough, from the Fish Pond reservoir alongside the East Ecton road to the dressing floors of the mine. Such a water supply was known as a 'launder'.

(8) Narrow Dale

Some 150 years ago this was a thriving community of 15 houses, of which the little that is left is in a state of decay.

(9) Alstonefield   See Walk 1.

Walk 9	Alstonefield - Narrow Dale - Hartington - Heathcote - Biggin - Biggin Dale - Peasland Rocks - Alstonefield.
	(9 miles)
Description	A relatively easy walk, only one steep climb, on the hillsides and tops around Wolfscote and Beresford Dales of the River Dove.
Map	OS Map Outdoor Leisure No. 24, scale 1:25000.
Start	Public car park, Alstonefield, ref. 131556.

Route

1. Turn left from the car park, cross road, then go right past grass triangle with seat, right again on to farm track, follow via stile/gate to field entrance, turn left alongside the wall and maintain the line across several stiled fields to a wall gap near disused barn.

2. Go through gap, turn right to cross wall stile and another in corner by trees, go half left to cross walled track via stiles, keep ahead across the field to pick up on left boundary wall, cross stile at its end.

3. Ahead is a wide grassy path which gradually descends to a wall stile, cross and go half left to bulge in facing wall, turn right on very short, rough descent to valley bottom, go left across stile/gate on to a track, the line of which is followed to the end of Beresford Lane at the River Dove.

This is the junction of Beresford Dale (left) and Wolfscote Dale (right).

4. Cross the footbridge; note the relatively uncommon design of the squeezer stile - finely worked to the proportions of a booted leg.

Follow the boundary wall up a track, cross stile then go left up a walled track to its junction with another, follow this left (the corner can be cut by field path if desired) round a bend, turn left on another through to a junction, go left, ignore side turns, through to Hartington[1], which is well served with pubs, cafés and shops.

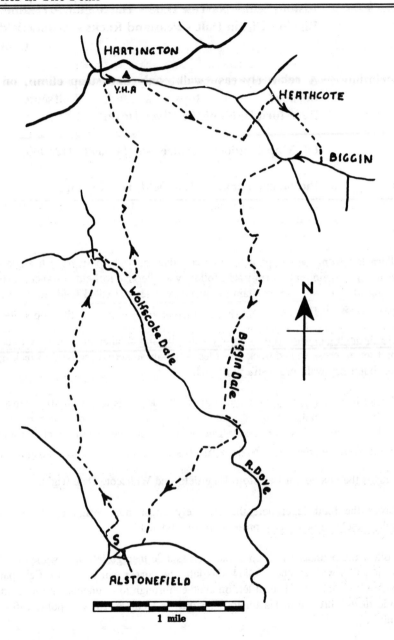

5. After visiting the village retrace steps to track end and continue up the road to yet another walled track *beyond* the Hall[2], now YHA; after approximately ¾ mile turn left, again on walled track to a road.

6. Cross stile opposite, ascend fields and pass through farmyard (ignore wall stile) to Heathcote's single street, turn right and follow to sharp bend.

7. Cross stile on clear path across three stiled fields to the grounds of Biggin Hall[3], pass through to the road through Biggin (Waterloo Inn just left), turn right to road junction, cross stile by signpost opposite on path which descends the full length of Biggin Dale. After passing sign for Hartington the path swings left to pass through a small gate, continues with wall on right, crosses a stile to continue with wall left, back again to the River Dove.

   The dale displays a good selection of wild flowers during spring and summer, and is a dry dale other than in times of excessive rainfall.

8. Turn left on riverside path, shortly thereafter crossing a stile; opposite old pumping station for Iron Tors, cross river by stepping stones; now comes the hard bit.

9. The path angles steeply up the hillside, via steps on the most difficult section, to a little plateau - a good spot for a breather and to admire the views; continue along the path, less demanding now, cross two stiles, the second one waymarked, go left, pass through gateway and on to wall corner stile.

10. Go along the wall to join a track near a barn, follow through to a junction, turn left, then, at the roadway ahead, turn right for Alstonefield[4], go past the village green with old coaching inn, The George, and turn right back to the car park.

Background Information

(1) Hartington	See Walk 15.
(2) Hartington Hall	See Walk 15.
(3) Biggin Hall	Early Georgian.
(4) Alstonefield	See Walk 1.

Walk 10	Monyash - Flagg - Chelmorton - Taddington - Sheldon - Monyash.
	(11 miles)
Description	Limestone uplands and villages mainly above the 1000 ft. level providing superb views.
Map	OS Map Outdoor Leisure No. 24, scale 1:25000.
Start	Monyash[1] car park, opposite chapel, ref. 149667.

Route

1. Leave the car park via the wall stile, go left round end of cottage, cross stile into field.

2. Go half left across a number of narrow clearly stiled fields and a walled track to a second track.

3. Turn right, follow track to a barn, ignore track left and stile ahead, carry on to end of track at walled-in gateway.

4. Cross stile, go half right, cross three stiles in line to farm drive, follow through to road.

5. Go along the road to the junction, Elizabethan Flagg Hall in grounds opposite, The Plough Inn to right, turn up Flagg's[2] single street to the small church.

6. Cross stile at footpath sign left, go half right, cross stile near trees, follow path, paralleling the street, up the fields, cross stile on to lane at Town Head.

7. Cross stile opposite, go round grassy mound, through gateway by trees, go half right, cross stile, one ahead at field corner and third by round topped tree, continue on a diagonal to cross far corner stile on to road.

8. Turn left, then second right down to footpath sign on left. An attractive view from here looking down on to Chelmorton[3], note the elongated S-shape of the narrow fields dating back to the medieval strip farming days; also much in evidence around Flagg and Taddington.

9. Descend field path to single street, turn right to the street end at church[4] and Church Inn with Chelmorton Low rising to 1470 ft. as backdrop.

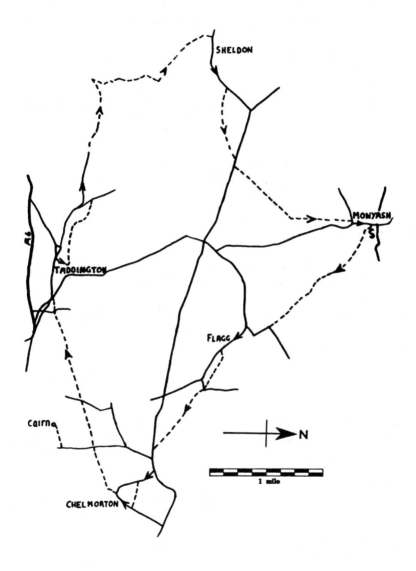

10. Continue up the rough track and along the path, past humps and hollows indicating the mining of a lead vein, to a track.

    A diversion to Five Wells[5] burial chamber can be made by turning left and following signs. Adds ¾ mile to walk distance.

11. Turn right, cross stile by footpath sign, go straight across field, continue on a straight stiled path across Taddington Moor to right corner of a reservoir.

12. Cross stile and another half right across field, take a line on church spire, descend fields to join worn path ending at stile and narrow road.

13. Cross road and stile opposite, at end of short path, cross stile, follow path between houses to road junction, follow road descending through Taddington[6]. Queen's Arms pub is on left.

14. Just before the road swings left to join the A6, turn right up walled track, go past its junction with one from right to another on left.

15. Follow this one, first descending, then ascending as it traverses across and up the hillside, at a junction near the top, go left to metalled lane.

16. Turn left then first right on to farm road, follow it, past Lodley View (house), straight to the end at a farm, cross waymarked stile right, turn left to descend Taddington Fields (if wet, some sections can be very muddy).

17. At the end of the wooded section, cross stile left and another in wall ahead, descend to junction with a left, right path.

18. Turn right on ascending path, waymarked numbers 2 and 3, follow number 3 route to stile at Great Shacklow Wood, do not cross, continue on short but steep ascent alongside wall, cross stile at top.

19. Go forward past short marker post, swing left alongside wall, cross corner stile, turn right as waymarked across two stiled fields to disused mine workings.

20. Turn left, follow straight line across several clearly stiled fields to waymarked stile, go as directed, right of further mine workings, cross broken gate on to

walled track, turn right, follow through into Sheldon[7].

A seat to left and one opposite are available for weary walkers and others.

21. Turn right, follow road through village, descend to second footpath sign (Flagg) on right, cross stile, go through gate in wall ahead and another by fenced square pond, keep left along line of telegraph poles, past another disused mine, to a stile.

22. Cross over, go slightly left to cross three more in line to a road, turn right then left down walled track, more mining evidence either side.

23. Cross stile at the end, follow waymarkers round wood, cross stile, follow markers down fields to road at Monyash, turn right then left back to car park.

Background Information

(1) Monyash (Maneis in Domesday Book - 'many ashes')

Granted market charter 1340, also date of market cross on village green.

Centre for sheep and cattle sales during fourteenth/fifteenth centuries.

Also important lead mining area and seat of Barmote Court which dealt with all legal matters concerning the mines.

Church of St Leonard originally dates from twelfth century of which parts remain.

(2) Flagg (Flageen in Domesday Book)

Strong local tradition that this was a Viking settlement. Note narrow strip fields behind cottages, dating from medieval times.

One time leadmining village, today best known for its Easter Tuesday point-to-point races and drystone walling contests.

(3) Chelmorton

A Saxon settlement but strangely not recorded in the Domesday Book. After Flash is second highest village (1100 ft.) in the country. Fine example of one street village with ancient crofts either side of the street behind each dwelling.

(4) Church

Probably England's highest parish church. The porch has a number of stone coffin lids, carved with swords, crosses and shields built into floor and walls. Oldest is twelfth century.

Parts of interior are Norman architecture, tower probably early thirteenth century.

(5) Five Wells Cairn

At 1400 ft., is the highest megalithic tomb in England, it is of the Neolithic (New Stone Age) era, some 4000 years old. Comprised of two stone burial chambers with passaged entrances covered by grassed over cairn of rubble about 70 ft. in diameter.

Thomas Bateman the famous or infamous Middleton by Youlgreave archæologist, untypically devoted a *whole* day (four in one day was his maximum) to explore the tomb in 1846. Contained twelve inhumations, flint tools and pottery fragments. Name derives from nearby five wells.

(6) Taddington (Tadintone in Domesday Book)

Saxon settlement, single street and narrow fields layout similar to Chelmorton.

Several narrow walled tracks go from street up hillside connecting with others crossing it, which in turn connect to old road and green lane to Monyash.

Probably used variously by villagers carrying water from High Well on the hillside, leadminers, cattle and sheep drovers to Monyash market.

Church - fourteenth century building on site of twelfth century chapel, one of two fonts is twelfth century.

(7) Sheldon (Sceladun in Domesday Book)

A prosperous leadmining village during eighteenth/nineteenth centuries. Most cottages and farmhouses date from late eighteenth century.

Walk 11	**Monyash - Sheldon - Over Haddon - Lathkill Dale - Monyash.**
	(10 miles)
Description	**Limestone uplands followed by one of the Peak District's most beautiful dales.**
Map	**OS Map Outdoor Leisure No. 24, scale 1:25000.**
Start	**Monyash car park, opposite chapel, ref. 150666.**

Route

1. Turn left from the car park, right at road junction then immediately left over a stile. The way ahead is well stiled and waymarked, passes right of clump of trees to a walled track, with evidence of lead mining left and right, and a road.

2. Go straight across on to a wide walled track, approximately 100 yds. down cross stile on right, angle slightly left across two fields to far left corner of second field, go half left to cross two more fields, then on a nearly straight line across four more to a wall outer corner.

3. Just beyond, cross stile on left and another immediately right, continue up the field to the road, turn left into Sheldon[1].

4. Walk through the village to a walled path by a telegraph pole, just below P. Gregory, Engineers. At the end of the walled path, cross two narrow fields, go diagonally across a third, follow wall side on to walled track.

5. At the bend, go left through wall gap (collapsed stile), keep straight ahead to visit the ruined buildings of the Magpie Lead Mine[2], a convenient drink stop.

6. Go back through the stile, follow right wall to a stile, cross over and follow a line to a thorn bush against right boundary wall, cross the stile, continue on the same line to a wall outer corner, go left along a track to the road in Kirk Dale.

7. Cross the stile opposite, climb the hillside to right edge of trees, follow waymarked route through gate and over stile, cross a field then follow left

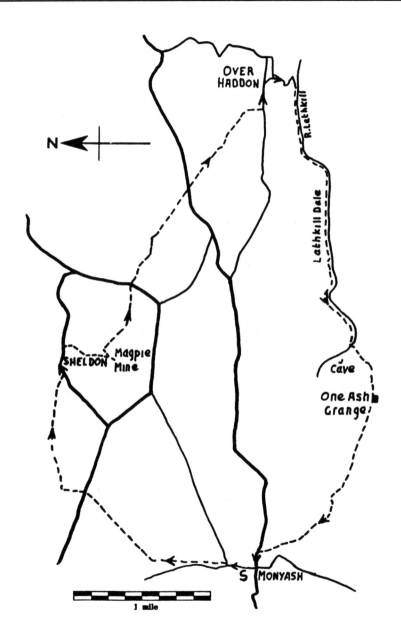

boundary down and along to corner stile, over this veer left on a straight line across three fields to the roadway.

8. Cross stile opposite, go diagonally across two fields, follow left boundary a little way, cross stile and on similar path line, cross three more stiles, last one near water trough, follow right boundary down to road at Over Haddon[3].

9. Turn left then first right down to public toilets and car park, small café and tea-room on left. (Lathkill Hotel is at far end of village street - not on route).

    Take the narrow lane, past the car park, descending steeply into Lathkill Dale, turn right near the bottom on broad path alongside the river, which, in these upper reaches, has little water in it during most of the year.

10. Note the separate and narrow water channel, close to the path, which carried the discharge from the Mandale Mine sough[4], the tail or outlet of which is a little further on, from where a path leads to the remains of the engine house, seen through the trees.

    Continue along the dale to the aqueduct pillars (1840) which supported a wooden trough carrying water from a leet on the south side of the river to the Mandale water-wheel. The line of the leet is still visible.

11. 300 yds. further on the left, is the site of a 52 ft. diameter water-wheel which worked six sets of 18 inch diameter pumps raising 4000 gallons/minute from a depth of 120 ft. in the Lathkill Dale Lead Mine.

12. The path next passes a weir and sluice gate; on the far side, is the source of the leet mentioned previously.

    At the end of the wooded section, once stood Carter's Mill, used for corn.

13. Continue up the dale, which now opens up to display the limestone faces, to a footbridge which the route crosses.

    (Those wishing to see Lathkill House Cave should carry on upstream for a few hundred yards. During periods of heavy rainfall the discharge of water can be quite spectacular; at other times there is but a trickle.)

14. From the footbridge, follow the path up and along the side of Cales Dale, cross the stile at the top, carry on up to One Ash Grange[5] yard; note the man-made 'cave', said to be used many years ago as a cold store, and also the ancient stone feeding troughs.

15. Go through the yard on to a track, where it turns into a field continue straight ahead alongside left boundary over two fields then cross to other side over two more fields.

16. Go half right to cross a stile, turn left and cross another on to a walled track, follow to a signpost, cross stile on right, go left alongside a wall and maintain this line through to churchyard and road in Monyash, tea-room and shop to the right.

17. Turn left past The Bull's Head pub and another little café, turn right at crossroads to car park.

Background Information

(1) Sheldon   See Walk 10.

(2) Magpie Mine

Most complete remains of a lead mine in the Peak District.

Worked intermittently for 300 years up to 1924. Three men killed in 1833 as a result of bitter disputes with rival miners from nearby mine over title to a lead vein.

The main shaft was 728 ft. deep and its principal sough (drainage channel) was driven one mile underground to the River Wye upstream of Ashford, where its tail (exit) can be seen discharging eight million gallons of water daily - a graphic illustration of the miners' problem with water in the mine.

(3) Over Haddon (Haduna in Domesday Book). Outlier of Bakewell.

'Over' distinguished it from 'Nether' which was depopulated when Haddon Hall grounds were extended in the Middle Ages.

(4) Mandale Mine and Sough

Mandale Mine existed from the thirteenth century. The sough built to drain the mine is over one mile long, started in 1797, finished in 1820.

One wall only remains of the engine house of 1847, behind which is a hollow for the earlier (1840) 35 ft. diameter water-wheel. Pumping shaft hole filled in.

In cliff face is 'inclined plane' mine entrance, with lead vein *in situ* above between limestone walls.

(5) One Ash Grange (Aneise in Domesday Book). Outlier of Bakewell.

Once a monastic grange farm owned by Roche Abbey, Yorkshire; used as a penitentiary for monks who had erred and strayed.

Farmhouse partly rebuilt. Quaker statesman John Bright (1811-99) honeymooned here.

(6) Monyash   See Walk 10.

Walk 12	Monyash - Sheldon - Over Haddon - Alport - Lathkill Dale - Monyash.
	(13 miles)
Description	An extension of Walk 11 taking in the delightful hamlet of Alport and the entire length of Lathkill Dale.
Map	OS Map Outdoor Leisure No. 24, scale 1:25000.
Start	Monyash car park, opposite chapel, ref. 150666 (as Walk 11).

Route

1. As Walk 11 to Over Haddon, at car park and toilets turn left along village street to Lathkill Hotel at very end.

2. Go to the front of the hotel and the stile at wall corner, take right one of two footpaths which goes half right across the hillside to an area of trees and scrub, cross two stiles then go straight ahead across a field, a road and two more fields to farm buildings.

3. Turn right through 'yard' on to a track (Dark Lane - part of the prehistoric route, The Old Portway), follow through to and across main road into Alport's[1] single street.

4. Descend to the river bridge[2] with an old mill[3] just downstream, turn right past the attractive houses and cottages of seventeenth and eighteenth centuries with their gardens across the road stretching down to the river side, also the early seventeenth century Monks Hall on left, rejoin main road at the later bridge of 1793.

5. The entrance to Bradford Dale is ahead left and that for Lathkill Dale is opposite across the road via a stile by a gate.

   Follow the field path to a road, turn right to cross Conksbury Bridge, built to carry the Newhaven to Grindleford turnpike, then go left on path through to Lathkill Lodge and rejoin the route of Walk 11 (end of paragraph 9, moving on to 10).

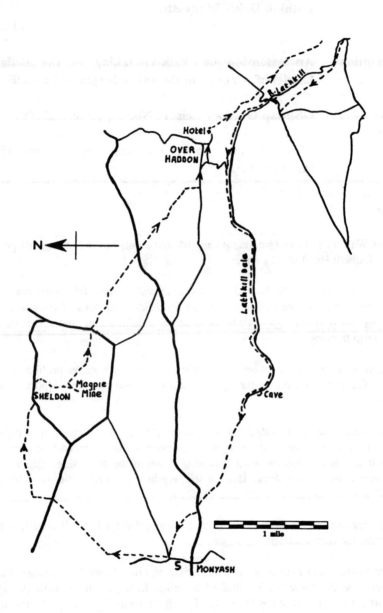

Hotel

OVER
HADDON

N

Lathkill Dale

Cave

Magpie
Mine

SHELDON

1 mile

S   MONYASH

6. Where that crosses the footbridge (Walk 11, paragraph 13), continue instead to follow the path up the dale past Lathkill House Cave, through a rocky section (part of the disused Ricklow Quarry) and along field path to road outside Monyash.

7. Either follow the road left into the village or, cross left to the signpost and stile and follow field path, curving left along field boundaries to a road junction, turn left for the car park.

Background Information

(1) Alport	See Walk 13.
(2) River Bridge	See Walk 13.
(3) Mill	See Walk 13.

Walk 13	Alport - Coal Pit Lane - Youlgreave - Bradford Dale - Elton - Harthill Moor - Alport.
	(9 miles)
Description	The beautiful dales of Lathkill and Bradford combined with higher level walking giving fine views plus interesting villages.
Map	OS Map Outdoor Leisure No. 24, scale 1:25000.
Start	Either side of road above Alport main road bridge, ref. 220646.

Route

1. Cross the bridge (1793), walk along Alport's[1] single street, passing the early seventeenth century Monks Hall (right) and other houses and cottages of seventeenth/eighteenth centuries to the second bridge[2] with an old mill[3] close by.

2. Turn left uphill, cross the main road on to Dark Lane, part of the south-east to north-west prehistoric 'Old Portway' (trade route), follow through to its end near barns, go left alongside fence to a footpath sign pointing back at an angle.

3. Follow the sign direction on to a path which zig-zags down through the trees to join a walled track - Coal Pit Lane (used by packhorses carrying coal from Chesterfield area), which crosses the River Lathkill near a trout farm, passes the early nineteenth century Rapers Lodge (used in the film of D. H. Lawrence's *Gipsy and the Virgin*) before ascending into Youlgreave[4], which is worthy of a look around before continuing.

4. Continue down the narrow road at side of Church[5], go right at fork descending steeply to the River Bradford. Ahead is Harthill Moor on the last section of the walk.

5. Turn right for a delightful riverside stroll through Bradford Dale, first on right bank then crossing to the left over a clapper bridge where a track comes down from Youlgreave.

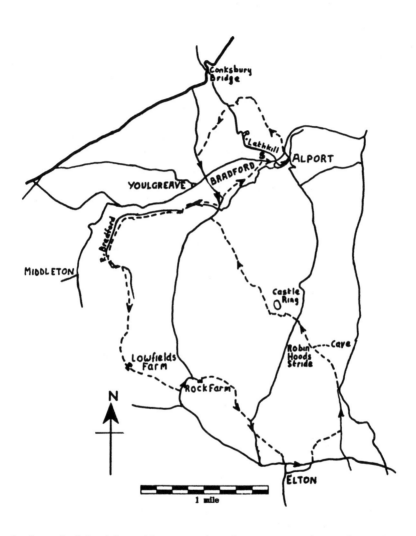

6. At the end of the dale, evidence remains of a water pumping station and a track leads up to Middleton.

Go left at track bottom, on a path, cross a footbridge, climb steps, go right to recross river and continue ahead, past a telegraph pole, on an easily seen, well stiled footpath across fields to a narrow lane.

7. Ignore stile opposite, instead follow the drive to Lowfields Farm, cross the yard via two gates, follow the left boundary to a stile, cross this to continue on the same path line across two more stiles, through a gate and Gratton Grange yard to a road.

8. Go left to a sharp bend, right at footpath sign, along Rock Farm drive, go through a gate, continue alongside wall to cross an area of trees via two stiles.

9. Bear right across three clearly stiled fields to pick up on left boundary wall, cross stile at the end, follow track by side of Anthony Hill, disused quarry[6], to the road below Elton.

10. Turn down the road, cross stile left, by footpath sign, climb diagonally to top left corner of second field, pass through gate to reach side road, turn right to main street in Elton[7], opposite Duke of York pub. Café in side road opens at weekends.

11. Walk down the village street, past the YHA (the Old Hall, late seventeenth century but much altered) to the sports ground, take the stiled footpath alongside, turn right at the end following a worn path across a stile then change direction to go slightly right across the slope, cross a wooden stile, not easily seen because of hedge, on to a lane.

12. Follow the lane downhill, cross the stile at the end, go up the farm track then the paved one (both lane and tracks are sections of the Old Portway) to Robin Hood's Stride also known as Mock Beggars Hall, an ideal break spot.

To the right are Crackcliff Rocks where there is a Hermit's Cave with a crucifix carved in the wall, antiquity unknown, may be fourteenth century. It can be found by following the path across the corner stile and round through the trees.

13. To continue the walk cross the adjacent stile, note the four large upright stones[8] to north, go diagonally across two fields, along the drive opposite to seventeenth century Harthill Moor Farm. The small hill at the back is known as Castle Ring, an Iron Age fort (protecting the Old Portway?).

14. Go left of the farm, cross a stile, swing right across two more stiles as the path crosses and descends the hillside, cross a stile on to a track.

15. Turn right then left as signed for Youlgreave on a distinct and easily followed field path back to the River Bradford.

16. There are two ways back to Alport and the car:

   a. Turn right and just follow the river side path, or,

   b. Go straight uphill to a sharp left hand bend, cross the stile right and the distinct path ahead leads to the road just above the car park. This way maintains the good views to the end.

Background Information

(1) Alport

Name derived from its position on the Old Portway; situated at the junction of rivers Bradford and Lathkill.

(2) Bridge

Built in 1718 to replace ford where impatient travellers, at times, had to wait up to ten days when high water levels made the ford impassable.

Draining of the many leadmines in the area, during later years will have significantly lowered water levels.

(3) Mill

Cornmill existed here at time of Domesday Book. Valued at five shillings and fourpence.

Referred to many times in Haddon Estate Charters, earliest

reference 1208. Buildings now hold trout rearing tanks.

(4) Youlgreave (Giolgrave in Domesday Book)

Second syllable may derive from 'grave' or 'groove', old miners' name for a lead vein, suggests mining taking place in eleventh century. Was centre of one of richest lead bearing areas of the Peak District.

YHA ex Co-operative shop built 1887. Opposite is Conduit Head, built 1829 for first public water supply.

Old Hall Farm 1630, Old Hall 1650.

(5) Church

Second largest in the Peak District after Tideswell and one of the most beautiful. Recorded in 1152 as being gifted to Abbey of St Mary, Leicester.

Experts date it at about 1130, south and north arcades are Norman. The size and beauty of the church reflects the early prosperity of the village.

(6) Anthony Hill

Grindstones from here exported to USA, Ghana and Alexandria for glass bevelling. Pulping stones to Scandinavia - paper making.

(7) Elton (Eltune in Domesday Book)

Saxon settlement adjacent to Old Portway, situated on limestone/gritstone border. Heavily mined for lead in limestone area (south) and quarried in gritstone (north).

Several good eighteenth century houses.

(8) Stones

Only four stones remain of the original nine in Bronze Age circle which, at 45 ft. diameter is second in size and importance in Derbyshire to Arbor Low.

Walk 14	**Alport - Over Haddon - Lathkill Lodge - Meadow Place Grange - Bradford Dale - Rock Farm - Anthony Hill - Mawstone Farm - Alport.**
	(9 miles)
Description	**Another excursion into the delightful area encompassing the beauty of the Lathkill and Bradford Dales.**
Map	**OS Map Outdoor Leisure No. 24, scale 1:25000.**
Start	**Roadside above Alport Road bridge, ref. 220646.**

Route

1. Cross the bridge (built 1793), walk along Alport's[1] single street with the early seventeenth century Monks Hall on the right; other houses and cottages are of seventeenth/eighteenth centuries.

   At the second bridge[2], note the old mill[3] before turning left up the hill to cross the main road on to Dark Lane, part of the prehistoric Old Portway (trade route).

2. Where the lane ends, continue to far end of barns, cross stile on left on to clear path line across two fields to a road.

3. Cross the field ahead, with fine views up Lathkill Dale, follow the stiled path along the edge of an area of trees and shrubs, then, on a right bearing, climb the fields to the white building (Lathkill Hotel) seen ahead.

4. Go past the front of the hotel, follow the road ahead through Over Haddon[4] to its end at a car park with toilets; refreshments are available nearby.

5. Turn left on the narrow lane descending steeply into Lathkill Dale; the building on the right at the bottom was once a mill, dating to 1529.

   Left by the riverside is Lathkill Lodge; the water pump in the garden covers an old lead mine shaft on a vein of lead that was worked under the river and up through the wood to the right.

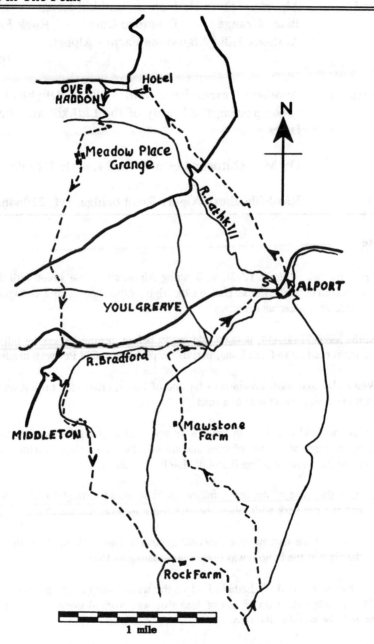

6. Cross the river by the footbridge - although for a large part of the year the river, in its upper reaches, disappears underground. Follow the zig-zag path up the hillside to a gate, turn left across the field and straight through the yard of Meadow Place Grange to a footpath junction and double signpost at the far side.

7. Take the right fork, signed for *Middleton*, follow the waymarkers up the field to cross a wall stile and another near left corner of next field; continue ahead to roadside stile.

8. Continue across the road on a clear path through disused lead vein workings to cross a narrow lane, then follow left boundary wall through several narrow fields, (with further evidence of lead mining) to the Youlgreave road.

9. Take the path opposite which descends to Middleton road, follow it right, past Lomberdale Hall[6] to a bend, leave at a signpost on a track descending into Bradford Dale and across the river bridge where once stood a corn mill.

10. Follow the river upstream to the end of the dale; here are the remains of a pumping station which provided spring water to the village of Middleton. At the bottom of the track up to the village, go left to cross a footbridge, ascend some steps, turn right and recross the river by clapper bridge.

11. Keep straight ahead past the telegraph post on a clearly stiled field path ending at a lane and the drive entrance to Lowfields Farm.

12. Turn left to cross stile/gate, ascend the fields, keeping right of a fenced area, to join a track ending at the lane above Gratton Grange.

    There may be two or three marshy sections which are easily negotiated by using the tufts of marsh grass as stepping stones.

13. Turn left then right along Rock Farm drive, go left of the farm alongside the boundary wall, through a small plantation, veer right across three stiled fields, then follow wall to a track past Anthony Hill quarry[7] (disused) to a road.

14. Turn left for 300 yards, cross stile on left, follow clear path line across fields and a farm drive to Tomlinson Wood, follow path round the wood to a three-way signpost at a gateway.

15. Pass through, turn left as signed for *Hopping Farm*, to another signpost, cross field half right as directed, to another post - *ignore its direction*; instead turn left alongside the wall, cross a stile and one opposite half right, continue through a gateway then a stile directly ahead on to a track.

16. Turn right to follow the track down to Mawstone Farm, go right at farm entrance by *PRIVATE* sign, follow field path indicated by signpost (remains of Mawstone Mine[8] are to the right), on to a track ending at a road.

17. Cross to a signpost, go up the field to junction with a crossing path, turn right along this path overlooking Bradford Dale, descending finally across a clapper bridge to the roadway.

18. Return to Alport, either by:-

    a) following riverside path, or,

    b) go up the wider of the two roads to a bend, cross stile on right, follow field path along hillside to reach the road just above the car park.

By maintaining height, b) gives pleasant views into the dale in addition to longer range ones.

Background Information

    (1) Alport   See Walk 13.
    (2) Second Bridge   See Walk 13.
    (3) Mill   See Walk 13.
    (4) Over Haddon   See Walk 11.

    (5) Meadow Place Grange

        Once a monastic farm in the ownership of Leicester Abbey.

(6) Lomberdale Hall

Home of Thomas Bateman, the famous (or infamous) nineteenth century archaeologist who, with his son William, excavated numerous burial cairns and barrows throughout Derbyshire.

He once did four in one day, tasks on which today's archaeologists would probably spend years.

(7) Anthony Hill   See Walk 13.

(8) Mawstone Mine

Closed in 1932 after exploding gas had killed five miners and three of the rescue party.

Walk 15	Hartington - Pilsbury Castle - Crowdecote - Longnor - Lower Boothlow - Hill End - Sheen - Hartington.
	(9½ miles)
Description	**A pleasing walk along the sides of the valleys of the Rivers Dove and Manifold in their upper reaches.**
Map	**OS Map Outdoor Leisure No. 24, scale 1:25000.**
Start	**Public car park, Hartington village centre, ref. 127604.**

Route

1. Take the minor road past pond and garage to just beyond its junction with gated road, turn right up walled track to roadway and Pilsbury signpost, go up the road as directed, cross wall stile at signpost.

2. The way is clearly marked up to ruined farm buildings, with fine views along the valley to the reef hills around Hollinsclough, here pass through the gateway, climb the slope left of the rock outcrop to a wall corner, keep ahead and cross wall stile, descend to footpath crossroads and Pilsbury signpost.

3. Go left as signed, past single standing stone (ancient waymarker?), cross old packhorse way (descending to ford the river at Pilsbury), continue over stiled fields on clear path to Pilsbury Castle[1].

   A plaque describes the castle and depicts what it was created for and how it may have looked.

4. After leaving the castle continue up through the riverside meadows, follow farm track through to Crowdecote[2]. The Packhorse Inn is not the original of packhorse days - that was the adjacent cottage.

5. Past the inn go left on Earl Sterndale road, left again at signpost, along farm drive to its end, continue straight ahead across fields, initially alongside boundary to reach a two-way signpost.

6. Turn left along a broad greenway, cross the infant River Dove, ascend the fields to a barn and rough road.

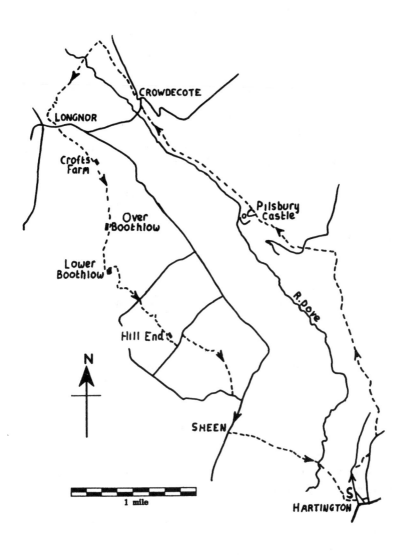

7. A short way up the road, cross stile right, follow zig-zag path, cross stile and field to a walled track, turn left at bottom, follow through to Market Place at Longnor[3] with its four inns, also a café, shop and toilets.

8. Turn left along Crowdecote road to farm drive and green footpath sign, turn left from farmyard centre, cross wall stile and narrow field to two-way signpost.

9. Take the path signed Croft and Over Boothlow (refreshments obtainable during 'season') over a number of clearly stiled narrow strip fields (date to medieval times), go straight through yard of Over Boothlow, then half right to cross stile and follow boundary towards Lower Boothlow.

10. Short of the farm, cross stile in left wall, walk round the buildings to join the farm drive through to the roadway.

11. Go through gate opposite and one in right wall, turn left along wall line to deep gully, go left a little way, cross footbridge, follow path alongside boundary to Hill End, pass right of the house via two stiles to the drive and road ahead.

12. Turn left then shortly right over field corner stile, go up the field and along the house drive, pass through gate on to path alongside wall, in second field veer left on shallow arc to stile in facing wall.

13. Cross to curved wall opposite, descend the fields via stiled path, go over a footbridge and ahead up next field to far right corner and nearby stile/gate.

14. Turn left down the lane to Manor Farm, then right on to road through Sheen[4], go past church and school to footpath sign at drive entrance to Ivy Cottage.

15. From the stile left, follow the path down the field, cross stile followed by footbridge, ascend the fields - the stiles can be seen ahead - go half right in last one before the ridge to stile/gate.

16. Ahead is a clear path, initially through a hollow way, follow this down the hillside, join stiled field path which swings right to road near cheese factory in Hartington[5], turn left back to car park.

Background Information

(1) Pilsbury Castle (Pilesberie in Domesday Book)

Finest 'motte and bailey' fortification in Derbyshire. Built to prevent further rebellions against William the Conqueror following those of 1068-9. Possibly continued in use until fourteenth century.

'Motte' - mound with timber barricade,
'Bailey' - defended courtyard for domestic buildings

(2) Crowdecote (Cruda's Cot in Domesday Book)

Cruda was a Saxon, 'cot' his humble shelter.

The Packhorse Inn has, inside, an old pack saddle with a row of tiny bells which gave warning of the packhorse train's approach.

The road was on the original packhorse way from Longnor to Bakewell.

(3) Longnor

Once an important market town with eight annual fairs. Note tariff board on front of the Market Hall (now craft centre), built in 1873.

Church is of 1780/81. Grave of William Billinge is in churchyard; it was claimed he lived to be 112 years old.

(4) Sheen (Sceon in Domesday Book)

The church, on site of medieval one, was built 1850-52 along with school, curate's house and Parsonage House with highly distinctive broad chimney stacks.

Sheen tug-of-war team has achieved world-wide reputation, having won National, European and World Championships at Youth and Senior levels. Formed in 1968 by local farmers.

(5) Hartington (Hortedun in Domesday Book)

Once a prosperous market town, now a tourist centre, popular with motorists and ramblers.

King John granted its market charter in 1203, the earliest in the Peak District. The Market Hall, now a shop, was built in 1836.

Hartington Hall, now YHA, is of 1611, modified in 1862.

Hartington is well known for Stilton cheese, manufacture of which was brought to the village by Leicester Stilton maker Mr. J. M. Nuttall.

Cheese shop is adjacent to village pond.

Walk 16	Longnor - Earl Sterndale - Dowel Dale - Washgate - Hollinsclough - Hardings Booth - Longnor.
	(9½ miles)
Description	One of the quieter walks, partly on ancient packhorse ways; takes in three interesting villages, varying views.
Map	OS Map Outdoor Leisure No. 24, scale 1:25000.
Start	Longnor Market Place (car parking), ref. 088649.

Route

1. Pass right of The Grapes Inn, straight over at the minor crossroads, turn right up walled track by a cottage, cross field via stiles, follow zig-zag path and track to barn.

2. Go left of the barn, straight ahead over fields, cross footbridge over infant River Dove on to wide greenway.

3. At the end, turn left along farm road to Underhill Farm, cross stile in wall and one opposite across the field, go ahead to large tree, veer left on faint track across the hillside to the wall side.

4. Follow wall round a corner, cross stile, go straight ahead to footpath sign, cross stile on right and descend fields to Quiet Woman pub at Earl Sterndale[1].

5. Turn left alongside wall and over three stiles, curve left to wall corner, ignore stile to right, continue left across two waymarked stiles, veer left down hillside path, across two more marked stiles to join roadway.

6. Turn right to Glutton Grange (1675)[2], go through yard and right on rough track, right again through a gate, ascend fields to another track.

7. Go left, with fine view of Chrome Hill ahead left, ascend to signpost right for Dowel Dale, cross field and descend to single track road.

8. A gradual ascent of the dale leads to the open moors with ever-widening views,

past a huge swallet (swallow hole) called Owl Hole. After approximately ¾ mile cross cattle grid and follow road left down to Booth Farm.

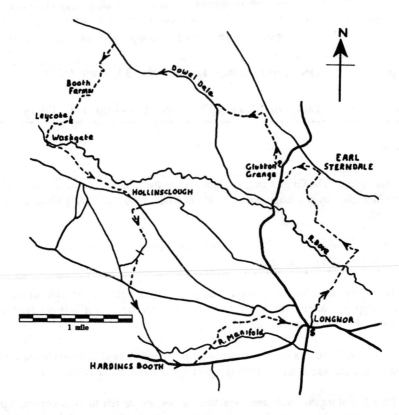

9. Go left from the yard on track down to Leycote, follow right then left to descend finally over a well preserved paved section to the beautiful setting of Washgate Bridge[3] over the River Dove, a crossing point of packhorse ways. This is an excellent lunch stop.

10. Cross the bridge and stile on left, follow well-trodden path across hillside, past a disused barn and rising to a broken wall, cross over and follow through to road at Hollinsclough[4] with fine views of reef hills Chrome and Parkhouse.

11. Just beyond the Chapel Hall, turn right onto another packhorse way, go left at junction on track, steadily climbing to join a metalled lane, go straight on at crossroads, cross stile on left by signpost, follow boundary through to a road.

12. Take the lane opposite for an enjoyable descent to a ford across the River Manifold and Hardings Booth, go left along the road to footpath sign by a gate.

13. Follow the path line ahead, across the Manifold by footbridge and on to the farm at Faurside across the valley, go through the yard, follow the path alongside the wall to stile/gate.

14. Veer slightly left down the field, cross footbridge and stile ahead, go right to stile at wall corner, follow left boundary wall through to farm road at Gauledge, continue along it back to market place at Longnor[5].

Background Information

(1) Earl Sterndale (not in Domesday Book)

'Earl' denotes it was originally in the ownership of the first Earl of Derby, as distinct from King Sterndale - in the ownership of the king.

Church built 1952 to replace nineteenth century one which was destroyed by enemy incendiary bombs during 1939-45 war: bombs probably intended for huge explosives dump near Buxton.

(2) Glutton Grange

One of the 50 or so ex-monastic farms within the Peak District.

'Glutton' derives from the largest member of the weasel family, the wolverine or glutton, a voracious predator found in Arctic or sub-Arctic regions.

(3) Washgate Bridge   See Walk 19.
(4) Hollinsclough   See Walk 19.
(5) Longnor   See Walk 15.

Walk 17	Parwich - Upper Moor Farm - Cobblers Nook Lane - Green Lane - High Peak Trail - Gallowlow Lane - Royston Grange - Parwich.
	(9 miles)
Description	A relatively easy, mainly high level walk, with good views. Takes in an interesting section of old railway and an ancient settlement.
Map	OS Map Outdoor Leisure No. 24, scale 1:25000.
Start	Roadside in Parwich, near church, ref. 187545.

Route

1. Take the road running NW from village centre, passing Parwich[1] Hall[2] on right, turn right opposite village shop, signed for Newhaven, then left at junction continuing to an acute left hand bend with stile on right.

2. Go up to left corner of the field, continue along a walled track, then ahead alongside the boundary wall to a gate, cross through to other side of wall and follow to some trees.

3. Cross stile on left and in a few yards cross back again to follow wall up the field to its end, keep straight ahead over the next three fields (via stiles, not gateways) to a corner stile at end of third.

4. Cross over to follow left boundary through trees to the far end of a narrow wood, bear slightly left on a straight line over the next three stiled fields, then follow right wall to a gate at the corner of a wood right of Uppermoor Farm.

5. Turn right alongside the wood to a walled track, Cobblers Nook Lane[3], go left at first bend, along field boundary then a walled track to a junction with two other lanes; Cardlemere ahead, Green right.

6. Follow Green Lane to its junction with the High Peak Trail[4], continue on the Trail past Gotham Bend[5] and Gotham Granges to Minninglow car park.

7. Carry on along the Trail with its very impressive limestone embankments, described by William Ruskin as 'vaster than the Walls of Babylon'; pass a disused quarry and lime kiln to the waymarked junction of Gallowlow Lane and the Trail; Minninglow Hill[6] is high to the left.

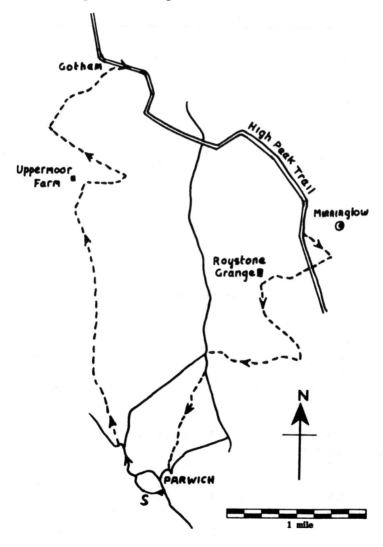

8. A short way up the lane cross stile right on to a path passing under the Trail and descending into the secluded valley of Roystone Grange[7]. Don't miss the stile left where the path crosses to far side of boundary wall.

9. Follow the waymarkers round to the Old Pumping House, taking time out to read about and inspect the excavated foundations of an earlier grange.

10. Leave the site on the track right, down the valley, turning right at a junction on to a signed path diversion past the devastation caused by Ballidon Quarry, returning to the track for a short distance; follow path left up hill, cross gate to join a road.

11. Turn left up the road to a signpost right, cross stile, go half left across two fields, left along next boundary then half right across three fields to wall corner. Follow clear path descending hillside through trees to a farm road.

12. Go down the road past the old Parwich hospital, now a home of rest, turn left at the junction then right and so back to the start.

Background Information

(1) Parwich (Puerewic in Domesday Book)

Granted a charter in AD 966 following the Great Council of AD 920, called by Edward the Elder (Alfred the Great's son) to unite the kingdom. Domesday Book refers to five manors including Parwich giving forty pounds of pure silver to the King. Silver ore usually associated with lead ore, suggesting leadmining in the area in the eleventh century.

Mesolithic (Middle Stone Age) man's presence in the area evidenced by finds of flint tools.

Church - built 1873 by H. Robinson of Derby incorporating earlier church original north doorway and chancel arch with Norman tympanum.

(2) Hall

Built 1747 by Sir Richard Levinge, whose use of brick instead of local stone has been described as 'a costly but effective piece of one-upmanship'.

(3) Cobblers Nook Lane

This lane along with Cardlemere, Minninglow and Gallowlow Lanes formed part of a packhorse route from Hartington to Wirksworth.

(4) High Peak Trail

Track bed of Cromford and High Peak Railway. Building started 1825, opened 1830, closed 1967. Connected Cromford Canal Wharf at 277 ft. above sea level to Peak Forest Canal, at Whaley Bridge, 517 ft. above sea level. Climbed to 1264 ft. over limestone plateau.

(5) Gotham Bend

The most acute bend of any public railway system in the country. Turned through 80° in a radius of 55 yards.

(6) Minninglow Hill

Surmounted by a small group of trees at around 1200 ft. above sea level, this is a Neolithic burial site consisting of a double-chambered stone tomb dating to third millenium BC. **NO PUBLIC ACCESS**.

(7) Roystone Grange

A decade of archæological research has shown the evolution over 6000 years from a pre-historic encampment, to a Roman mining village then a Cistercian (Garenden Abbey, Leicestershire) Grange sheep ranch and finally a hill farm.

The full details of the dig are given in the book *Wall to Wall History* by Richard Hodges, published by Gerald Duckworth & Co. Ltd.

Walk 18	Tissington - Spend Lane - Bostern Grange - Alsop-En-Le-Dale - Parwich - Lea Hall - Tissington.
	(10 miles)
Description	A walk in the limestone foothills, including three interesting villages. Fine views throughout.
Map	OS Map Outdoor Leisure No. 24, scale 1:25000.
Start	Tissington[1] - old railway station, ref. 177521.

Route

1. Turn left out of the car park, pass the pond, take the driveway out of the village, keep straight ahead where drive swings left. Cross two stiles, angle left to a stile and roadway (A515).

2. Cross stile and field opposite, along medieval ridge and furrows, cross second stile, go diagonally across field, left through wall gap, right over wall stile, ascend hillside to Spend Lane - part of eighteenth century coach route from Derby to Manchester.

3. Go over stile opposite, follow path to three-way footpath sign, cross stile, go left through gateway to follow clearly stiled and waymarked path to Bostern Grange (monastic sheep farm before dissolution of monasteries). *En route* a disused lime kiln with explanatory plaque is on left just beyond spinney.

4. Go through the yard, straight ahead across three fields, turn left at wall (signed for Milldale), in next field turn right down Hanson Grange Drive, cross minor road to field right corner stile.

5. Cross major road to car park, once Alsop Station on Ashbourne to Buxton railway, turn left on to Tissington Trail (railway track bed) then immediately right to descend fields along boundary, crossing stile part way down, to other side of wall.

6. At the lane turn right to walk through Alsop[2], cross stile left at corner of cottage garden, go half right across two signed stiles then right on path through wood.

7. Follow field wall at start of clearly stiled way down the fields to a farm drive, cross to stile near field far right corner, cross second farm drive and another stile to reach Parwich road via a gate at end of third drive.

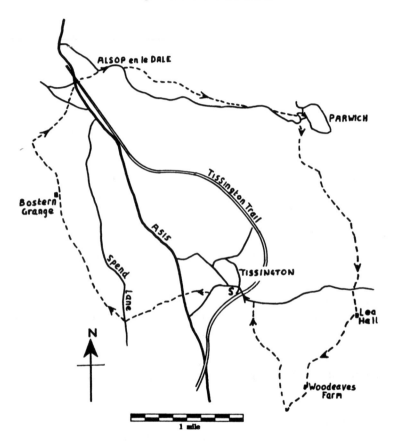

8. Turn left for Parwich[3], after approximately 400 yards go up track, forward left, cross stile on to clear stiled path across narrow fields to road in Parwich.

9. Follow the minor road past the school, the large brick building is Parwich Hall, turn right along major road past village shop (open Sundays), go right at the green, to reach a stream. The pub is a few yards further on left.

10. Turn right on path alongside stream, turn left as signed for Tissington, cross two stiled fields, go half left, in third cross wall stile and another in next field corner.

11. Go left through gap, right alongside the boundary across two fields, bear right at end of wall in third field, cross stile in right wall of fourth, curve left to follow stiled path along boundary hedge down and across several fields to a gateway.

12. Pass through, follow right fence, cross footbridge, keep ahead to cross stile adjacent to and partly obscured by a tree.

13. Maintain the same path line to the brow of the hill, descend to cross hedge stile, follow right boundary and cross corner stile to road from Tissington village to the ford.

14. Go down Lea Cottage Farm drive, through the yard, up the track with Lea Hall below left, pass through gateway, follow right boundary to a stream at wood corner, via a gate and stile.

15. Cross stream, go half left across the slope to an area of scrub, keep top side, descend, no defined path, to ford stream, go half left through gateway and across field to reach Woodeaves Farm.

16. Leave by the drive, after approximately 50 yards cross wooden stile right to ascend fields, initially alongside the hedge across two stiles then straight ahead across a third by a wood to field corner.

17. Turn left, cross another stile, angle right, pass through a gate and another ahead to an estate road, go straight ahead to T-junction, turn left back to car park.

Background Information

(1) Tissington (Tizington in Domesday Book)

An estate village owned by the Fitzherberts since 1462; the hall dates from the seventeenth century.

The village is famous for the dressing of its five wells which takes place each year on Ascension Day. Origins lost in antiquity, believed by some to be pagan. First formally recorded in 1758.

Church - Much of it is Norman but *not* the Normanised north aisle added in 1854. The font is considered to be early Norman.

(2) Alsop-en-le-Dale (Elleshope in Domesday Book)

The Alsops came into possession from William Ferrers, Earl of Derby, in late thirteenth century and lived here until late seventeenth century.

Hall - seventeenth century with nearby farm buildings of seventeenth/eighteenth century.

Church - Much of it is Norman but present tower dates from 1883.

(3) Parwich   See Walk 17.

Walk 19	Hollinsclough - Hollinsclough Moor - Thick Withins - Wickenlow - Blackbank - Wilson Knowl - Wildstone Rock - Far Brook - Three Shire Heads - Ready Leech Green - Axe Edge End - Nether Colshaw - Washgate - Hollinsclough.
	(10 miles)
Description	A quiet moorland walk with magnicient long ranging views. Best in spring with curlews and skylarks for company or late summer with heather in full bloom.
Map	OS Map Outdoor Leisure No. 24, scale 1:25000.
Start	Roadside in Hollinsclough, ref. 065665.

Route

1. Follow the old packhorse trail, left of the Chapel[1] Hall, which climbs the hillside (ignore left turn) to a minor road then goes right and left on to a walled track to cross Hollinsclough Moor on to Longnor to Flash road.

2. Turn right and just beyond road junction, cross stile on left, go forward a few yards then right on a faint path raking down the hillside to a corner stile in a marshy area; easy to negotiate.

3. Keep right to circumnavigate another marshy section, cross a stream by footbridge on to Thick Withins Farm drive via a stile.

4. Go through the farmyard on a gated track, at its end cross a stile and field, pass through Sunnydale Farm and cross a stream.

5. Turn right, follow the stream, keeping initially to the high ground, after crossing four field boundaries, cross the stream at a convenient point, go half right to Wicken Low, cross wall stile into yard, follow drive to a minor road.

6. Cross the stile opposite, keep straight ahead up the field to a raised path, follow left to a footbridge (on left at the path end); after crossing, angle right up the field to a stile left of Blackbank buildings, follow track to A53 (Leek to Buxton).

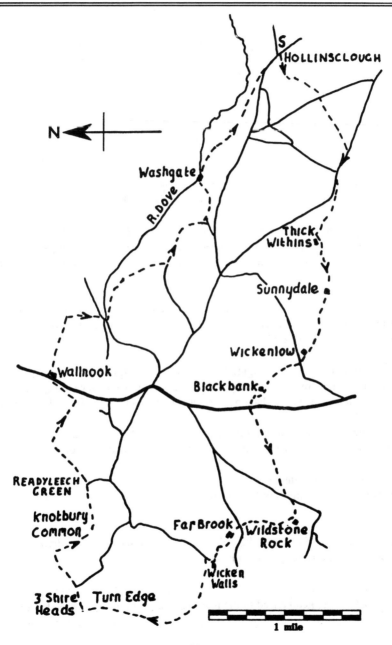

N

S

HOLLINSCLOUGH

Washgate

R. Dove

Thick Withins

Sunnydale

Wickenlow

Wallnook

Blackbank

READYLEECH GREEN

Knotbury Common

FarBrook

Wildstone Rock

Wicken Walls

3 Shire Heads   Turn Edge

1 mile

79

7. Cross the road and stiles opposite, go half left to another, keep straight ahead across a footbridge and the next stile can be seen right of farm buildings of Wilson Knowl at the side of farm drive.

8. At the drive look ahead to see two wall squeezer stiles and beyond, a roadside footpath sign. A rough area on the direct line is best avoided by taking a right hand curve which crosses a steepish narrow ditch, looks worse than it really is.

9. Having reached the road, follow the track opposite through Wildstone Rock Farm to the end of a walled track, turn right along the field boundary, go through a gate and follow left boundary past a house to the Flash to Allgreave road.

10. Turn right then left down the steep drive to Far Brook Farm (a very friendly welcome here if you stop to buy refreshments), pass through the gate on to the bridleway (old packhorse trail) turning left, as signed at the footpath crossroads, for Three Shire Heads.

11. Go via Wicken Walls Farm drive on to a track swinging left round Turn Edge Hill and down to the attractive Panniers Pool and Three Shire Heads[2] (a very popular refreshment stop).

12. Pass through the gate on right, follow a track, alongside a stream, to a minor road, turn right by footpath sign, up a track over Knotbury Common, cross a ladder stile at a bend, go diagonally right across two fields to Readyleech Green.

13. Continue along the farm road opposite, at far end of the second house, turn right and aim for left corner of field on the hillside with a fence stile on left.

14. Cross stile, turn right to join track at Axe Edge End, swing left down to A53, cross the road, go through Wallnook Farm and straight down the fields to a farm road.

15. Go right over a stile, along the little valley to a house, follow its drive to a road, turn right to a footpath sign on left, cross stile to a stiled path skirting field boundaries.

16. At a metal gate, keep ahead to the line of trees, go right, over a ladder stile, turn

half left to a visible wooden stile and on the same line, cross several fields to a farm road.

17. Pass through the gate adjacent to finger post, descend field, turn left at wall corner, cross stile on to overgrown walled track.

18. Turn right to a little dip in the now metalled track, cross stile on left, reach a house via a small gate, turn right then immediately left on a path which joins the packhorse way descending to the evocative setting of Washgate Bridge[3].

19. Do not cross, instead go over stile ahead, follow well-worn path along the hillside, above the River Dove, after passing in front of disused barn, keep ahead to pick up on a broken wall to right.

20. The path is on far side of the wall and after crossing a wooden stile continues as a wide grassy path, the nearness ahead of the reef hills Chrome (Chroom) and Parkhouse indicates Hollinsclough[4] and journey's end, reached via a short walled track and left turn down the road.

Background Information

(1) Chapel (Bethel)

Built 1801, in his garden by John Lomas - a jaggerman (leader of packhorse train).

(2) Three Shire Heads

The boundaries of Cheshire, Staffordshire and Derbyshire meet here. Several packhorse ways crossed at this remote spot tucked away between the moorland hills in the upper reaches of the River Dane.

Site of prize fights and cock fights, and a haunt of outlaws who could escape across the appropriate county boundary should the law arrive.

(3) Washgate Bridge

Bridge on the road to the wash - Gate from *gata* - Danish for road.

Sheep were washed here by driving them across the River Dove.

An excellent example of a minor packhorse bridge with parapets only some 15 inches high to allow clearance for panniers. Walkway approximately four feet wide.

Fine example also, of paving on the bridge itself and up the steep track on Derbyshire side.

(4) Hollinsclough (not in Domesday Book)

Unspoilt hamlet situated on packhorse routes. Once famous for its silk-weaving cottage industry.

The conical limestone reef hills of Chrome and Parkhouse were formed some 350 million years ago when the area was covered by a shallow tropical sea.

Walk 20	Errwood Reservoir - Errwood Hall Ruins - Shining Tor - Pym Chair - Windgather Rocks - Overton Hall Farm - Fernilee Reservoir - Errwood Reservoir
	(9 miles)
Description	A fine moorland ridge walk with an easy finish alongside the reservoirs.
Map	OS Map Outdoor Leisure No. 24, scale 1:25000.
Start	Public car park at Errwood Reservoir, ref. 012747.

Route

1. Take the path from the back of the car park, up the slope and through a pedestrian gap in the wall on to a rhododendron and tree lined path in the extensive grounds of the former Errwood Hall[1].

   40,000 rhododendron bushes were planted by the owner; they present a magnificent sight when in bloom.

2. Follow the path to just short of *Woodland Walk* sign, ascend steps on to another path leading right to the hall ruins.

3. Leave on red waymarked route along a path which passes between stone pillars to rejoin original path, follow to opening between stone gate posts.

   A path to the right leads to the Grimshaws' private burial ground.

4. To continue the walk turn left by the wall on a path which crosses a stream then zig-zags up the hillside to a ladder stile; over this, turn right on a steady ascent to cross a stile by a gate signed *1 Shining Tor to Pym Chair*.

5. Follow the path to Shining Tor and the start of the ridge walk along what is the boundary of Derbyshire and Cheshire.

   The path passes The Tors, Cats Tor and Oldgate Nick (where packhorse trains carrying salt from Cheshire crossed the ridge, after fording Todd Brook, near *Salters*ford Hall, due west), to arrive at Pym Chair and the road (Roman route).

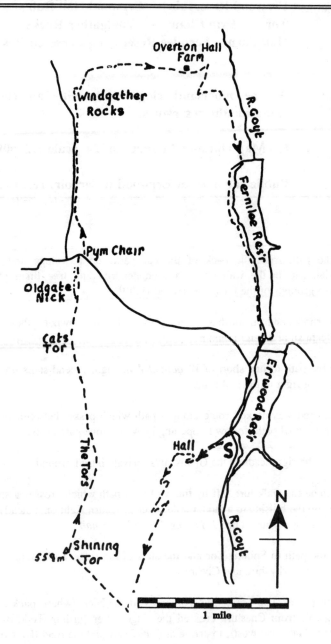

Overton Hall Farm

Windgather Rocks

R. Goyt

Fernilee Res'r

Pym Chair

Oldgate Nick

Cats Tor

Errwood Res'r

The Tors

Hall

S

N

R. Goyt

559m

Shining Tor

1 mile

The chair-shaped stone with initials 'PC' inscribed is long gone - only the name remains.

6. Over the road, cross fence stile by signpost for *Windgather Rocks*, follow the path through the heather and over a ladder stile at far end.

7. Continue on the path past the rocks (popular with climbers), cross a ladder stile on to a path descending to, then alongside a wood to cross a second ladder stile, turn right as waymarked along a path through the trees to cross a third stile.

8. Looking from the top of the rise ahead, the town of Whaley Bridge lies down below to the left.

   Follow the path down the moor, along the farm drive opposite, go past the buildings, round a hairpin bend and past Madscar Farm, cross a stream, go through pedestrian gate and continue past Knipe Farm on a track along the valley side, with the River Goyt below, to its junction with a road at Fernilee Reservoir[2] Dam.

9. Turn right along the the road then left over a stile on to a tree lined path, go left at a junction waymarked *3* where the path continues alongside the reservoir; follow it until nearing the Errwood Dam then angle right along a path as indicated by waymarking arrow *3*.

10. Where this path ends continue ahead to join the road alongside Errwood Reservoir[3] and so back to the car park.

Background Information

(1) Errwood Hall

Built in 1830 for Samuel Grimshaw who entertained on a grand scale and had a large staff of foreign servants.

The children of the Hall were educated by a Spanish aristocrat, Dolores de Bergrin, Mrs Grimshaw's personal companion, who inspired

85

such affection that, on her death, a shrine to her was built at the side of the minor road from the A5004 down to Errwood Dam.

The estate had its own coal mine and the Grimshaws owned an ocean-going yacht whose captain is buried in the family graveyard.

(2) Fernilee Reservoir

Completed in 1938 for Stockport Corporation.

(3) Errwood Reservoir

Completed in 1967.

The packhorse bridge over the River Goyt, on the route of the old Roman road up to Pym Chair, was dismantled and rebuilt one mile downstream.

Walk 21	Wetton Mill - Butterton - Onecote - Ford - Felthouse - Grindon - Ossom's Hill - Wetton Mill.
	(9 miles)
Description	Takes in some quieter ways, not too strenuous, with pleasing views, particularly around Grindon and Ossom's Hill.
Map	OS Map Outdoor Leisure No. 24, scale 1:25000.
Start	Public car park, Wetton Mill on Manifold Trail, ref. 094561.

Route

1. Go left from the car park then right through a gate along a path which, further on, joins the right bank of Hoo Brook.

2. Follow upstream to a junction of five ways, take the one at 45° right to continue alongside the brook to a signpost, cross to other side and continue upstream on left bank to Butterton[1].

3. In the last field, go right across stile and brook on to a track, turn left and cross the ford to an open area left of a cottage.

4. Climb the stone steps at the back of this area, follow walled track into field, go left alongside wall then keep ahead across several clearly stiled narrow fields to deserted farm buildings.

5. Continue straight ahead up the hill on to farm drive, follow through to roadway, cross on to Grindon Moor on a clear path across and descend (follow line of telegraph poles) to a stile right of a gate.

6. Carry on down farm drive to road above Onecote, near to seventeenth century Old Hall, cross stile opposite and one in wall ahead; shortly beyond, turn left through hedge gap, cross field and stile on to a track, go right a short way then cross left to centre of trees and a footbridge.

7. Cross over and into Onecote Grange yard via a gate, leave along the drive which crosses the River Hamps to a lane, go left, past the church, cut a corner by taking path past village hall to the main road in Onecote[2].

The Jervis Arms pub is to left.

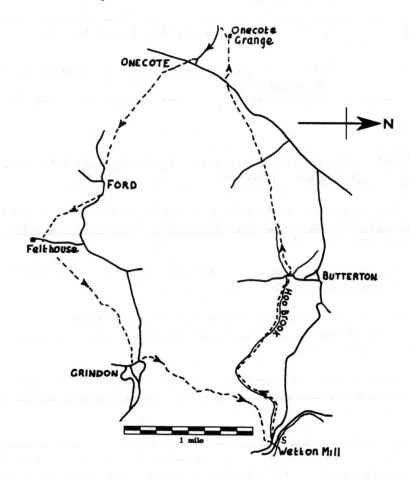

8. Cross right to signpost and stile, go slightly left to cross second stile, turn right on easily followed path along boundaries across several fields before angling left

in last two to the buildings of Banktop Farm, seen ahead at Ford.

9. Leave by the farm drive, cross the bridge over the River Hamps, turn right along the road through Ford to wall stile on right.

10. The route goes along the field gradually dropping down to meet a track, turn left along the boundary and cross a footbridge in the corner, which may be hidden from view when foliage is in full leaf.

11. Continue along the embankment of what was once a mill-pond to the sad ruins of an old corn mill which served the Ford estate, pass right of the ruins to a house, follow driveway through to a roadway.

    The house owners, over a number of years, have (and are still doing so) made great efforts to restore the mill stream and recreate the pond. Unfortunately the mill is too far gone for their limited resources.

12. Cross the stile opposite right by footpath sign, pass through hedge gap ahead adjacent to electricity pole with transformer, follow a line parallel with telegraph poles and cross footbridge and stile near creeper covered tree.

13. Maintain the same line to trees at a wall corner, continue on a line between gatepost and trees, cross stile at far side of field, go half right and cross another at a gate.

14. Turn left along the boundary, cross two stiles and, shortly, a third in the left boundary. Grindon Church can now be seen ahead.

15. Aim a little to right of church, cross double stile, follow right boundary and cross stile on to road in Grindon[3] adjacent to The Cavalier Inn, sixteenth century building which was an undertakers prior to becoming an inn - reputed to have a resident ghost.

16. Turn left, take the farm road between church and picnic area. Near its end turn left towards a farm, pass right of the buildings, as signposted, across stiled fields to the footpath along the tree line to Ossom's Hill from where the view is magnificent.

17. At the end of the trees, turn left and descend across Hoo Brook back to car park and Wetton Mill[4].

Background Information

(1) Butterton   See Walk 22.

(2) Onecote

Pronounced *on-cut*. Lies in the wide valley of the upper River Hamps.

The church dates from 1753 and contains a canopied pulpit, also boards with The Ten Commandments which were erected in 1755.

Two miles north, at grid reference 045574 are the remains of the Mixon Copper Mine, closed late nineteenth century.

(3) Grindon (Grendone in Domesday Book)

Sits on the East Staffordshire moors at 1000ft. above sea level overlooking the Manifold Valley.

The church register dates from 1697 but present church is of 1848. Inside is a framed Calvary tapestry and plaque commemorating six airmen who died when their Halifax plane crashed in a blizzard on Grindon Moor while parachuting supplies to villages of the area cut off during the great snows of 1947.

(4) Wetton Mill   See Walk 22.

Walk 22	**Wetton Mill - Sugar Loaf - Ecton - Warslow - Upper Elkstone - Butterton - Wetton Mill.**
	(9 miles)
Description	**Covers part of the scenically impressive Manifold Valley and quieter ways of East Staffordshire moorlands.**
Map	**OS Map Outdoor Leisure No. 24, scale 1:25000.**
Start	**Public car park Wetton Mill, ref. 084561.**

Route

1. Cross the river bridge, go left on the track to Dale Farm, continue past the farm on a clear path ascending the hillside past Sugar Loaf (small hill) ending at farm road.

2. Pass through the gate just ahead on left, follow wall up the field to an opening, go diagonally across two fields, follow wall on left, cross stile at crest of hill.

3. Continue ahead for several yards to meet path traversing the hillside, turn right and follow through to odd looking house[1] with green, copper spire, adjacent to remains of Ecton Hill copper mine[2].

4. Follow the road down to the river, cross the bridge, go up the road to signpost left, cross stile, go half left up hillside, cross squeezer stile - hidden by bushes.

5. Turn right, pass through wall gap, go up field on diagonal, cross wall stile, follow right boundary, go half left near farm, cross farmhouse ground via two stiles to road at Warslow[3], shop to right.

6. Turn left, first right up village street past Greyhound Inn and camping barn to a bend, leave road, continue along rough track to a sharp turn - gate facing.

7. Pass through gate, keep straight ahead, cross footbridge, go half left to stile, cross over, follow right boundary through to a road.

8. Cross right to signpost, angle right as directed, follow left boundary to its end,

cross open area ahead, join farm track.

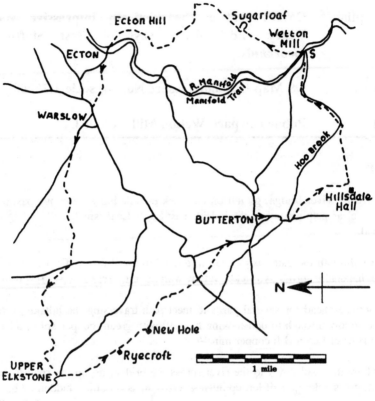

9. Follow left to gate with waymarker disc (track bends left here down to farm), turn right to similarly marked gate, go through, turn left to cross waymarked stile at wood.

10. Follow path descending steeply through the wood, cross footbridge, go straight ahead across field, cross stile on walled track through to road in Upper Elkstone[4].

11. Turn down the road to a bend, go right on track, past the church and Mount Pleasant Farm, to its end, turn through gate on right, continue on same line as track, alongside left boundary, cross footbridge, ascend field to

Ryecroft Farm.

12. Cross two stiles in line, finger post indicates Butterton route, follow white arrows round farm buildings, cross stile, little brook, and footbridge ahead left.

13. Follow boundary to farm track, cross stile left of gate marked private, follow re-routed path to New Hole Farm drive, turn left to signpost, cross little boggy section (walk the tufts), follow path line gradually rising across hillside, cross hedge stile.

14. Keep ahead to join wide grassy path (original bridle path is hollow way below left) then wide track, follow across brook alongside wall, swing right along stony hollow way, cross stile on to farm track.

15. Pass Butterton sign and two small barns, descend bank through small gate, cross brook, ascend field to Onecote - Warslow road.

16 Go straight across, follow right boundary to its end, angle slightly left, cross two stiled fields to road above Butterton[5].

17. Turn right, left at the junction (shop and off-licence along here), left at the fork, right at next junction to pass church and Black Lion Inn (1782), descend to ford where Hoo Brook crosses the road.

18. Continue up the road to stile/gate on left, follow the track to wall corner, go half right in straight line across two stiles and footbridge, follow right boundary to Hillsdale Hall.

19. At signpost short of gate, cross wall stile, follow stiled/gated path down fields, cross brook at bottom, turn left and follow Hoo Brook back to Wetton Mill[6].

Background Information

(1) House

Built 1933 by Arthur Radcliffe, Conservative MP for Leek, notorious for his virtual non-attendance at the House of Commons.

(2) Ecton Copper Mine

First dated reference to mining activity was 1654. A rich 'pipe' of copper was mined to a depth of 1400ft. Most productive period was eighteenth century, the owner, Duke of Devonshire, had profit of £300,000 enabling him to build The Crescent at Buxton.

(3) Warslow (Wereslei in Domesday Book)

Formerly estate village of Harpur-Crewe family of Calke Abbey, near Melbourne, Derbyshire. Warslow Hall was their shooting lodge - still owned by family.

(4) Upper Elkstone (not in Domesday Book)

Church built 1786 has box pews, gallery, two-decker pulpit with tester (canopy). Also royal arms of George III.

(5) Butterton (not in Domesday Book)

A pleasant village set 1000ft. above sea level, spire of 1871 church is landmark for miles. Some houses date from seventeenth and nineteenth centuries.

(6) Wetton Mill

Mill established by William Cavendish, second son of Bess of Hardwick; belonged to Dukes of Devonshire until about 1617. Finally abandoned 1857.

Wetton Mill Minor Rock Shelter revealed artefacts from all periods, Mesolithic to Bronze Age.

This stretch of the valley is very rich in terms of prehistoric finds excavated from several caves or rock shelters.

A little downstream of mill, River Manifold disappears underground during dry season, reappearing four miles away at Ilam Boil Holes (see Walk 1).

<table>
<tr><td>**Walk 23**</td><td>**Rushton Spencer - Weathercock Farm - Hollinhall - Danebridge - Wincle Grange - Nettlebeds - Nabbs Hill - Wincle Minn - Barleighford Bridge - Rushton Spencer.**
(10 miles)</td></tr>
<tr><td>**Description**</td><td>**A mix of wooded valleys of river and streams, with high level walking and very attractive views.**</td></tr>
<tr><td>**Map**</td><td>**OS Map Outdoor Leisure No. 24, scale 1:25000.**</td></tr>
<tr><td>**Start**</td><td>**Car park at old railway station by Knot Inn, Rushton, ref. 935624.**</td></tr>
</table>

Route

1. Turn right from the car park, cross the main road, go first right up a drive across the feeder stream[1], keep left of the buildings and pass through a gate on to field path.

2. The way ahead is clearly stiled; after breasting a rise, make for the house seen ahead, cross stiles in field corner to minor crossroads.

3. Go straight across and up towards house, cross stile on right, pass buildings to wall stile, keep ahead to cross boundary at junction of fence and hedge, turn left to squeezer stile then immediately right over another, follow right boundary to reach a track.

4. Follow to its end at a farm, turn right in the yard through a gate, go left on a line right of line of trees and a single tree further on. Ahead can be seen the huge mound of Shutlingsloe (limestone reef hill), while, to the left, are the PO communications tower at Bosley and excellent views of wooded valleys.

5. Cross fence stile, veer a little left to another, cross stream by footbridge, ascend to Hollinhall Farm and three-way signpost, go through yard as signed for *Danebridge*, follow yellow waymarker (ignore large red arrow) across a stile, continue as directed, across the field and another stile on to path which swings left to descend to a footbridge over the River Dane.

Up to the right is the start of the feeder stream.

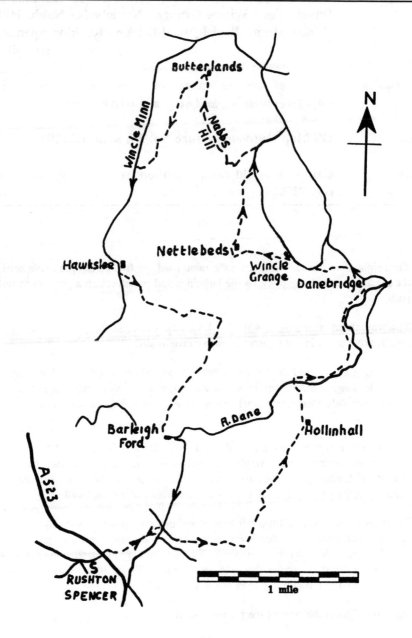

N

Butterlands

Wincle Minn

Nabbs Hill

Hawkslee

Nettlebeds

Wincle Grange

Danebridge

R. Dane

Barleigh Ford

Hollinhall

A 523

S
RUSHTON
SPENCER

1 mile

6. Cross the bridge to follow the path across the riverside meadows to a trout farm and lake, cross stile on left and ascend to road above Danebridge, turn left to just beyond the Ship Inn, cross stile left and one across field, continue over a drive up the field to corner stile.

7. Follow the path uphill through the trees, cross two stiles in line on to narrow lane, turn left to just short of the main buildings of Wincle Grange[2], go left through gateway and three gates closely in line to cross a stile.

8. The next stile is ahead at the end of trees; continue as waymarked, cross stile, turn right and pass through the farmyard to the drive, leave half left to join the boundary hedge up the field, follow it to cross a stile and a second immediately right.

9. Continue past house alongside left boundary; where it swings left keep ahead to cross wall gap just right of four trees, follow path line right to cross stile on to narrow lane at a cottage.

10. Go left to a farm drive, turn left off this as waymarked, follow farm track downhill and round sharp bend, cross stile right at a signpost, go straight ahead to stile in left boundary fence, follow path down valley side, cross stream.

11. The next stile is directly ahead over the top of the wooded hill; a number of large fallen trees necessitates a bit of a detour.

    Follow the obvious path for about 30 yards, turn sharply left up the hill, then left again across the hillside, to clear the fallen trees, on to a well worn path swinging right to cross the stile.

12. Continue along the ridge of Nabbs Hill on a steady ascent to a double gateway (the view makes the climb worthwhile), pass through the right hand gateway, follow the boundary to a farm track.

13. Go left along the track, through several bends to where it ends at a line of trees, continue ahead across the fields on a slight right bearing to cross a waymarked stile/gate, pass through gate ahead and along wall side to drive of Higher Greasley Farm, follow up to gated road along Wincle Minn, part of the Gritstone Trail.

14. Follow the road left to just beyond Hawkslee Farm, turn left at Trail signpost, cross waymarked stile (direction indicated is too much right), take telegraph pole ahead as a guide, cross field corner stile, keep ahead to broken boundary and follow to join waymarked track.

15. The way ahead is clearly marked as it descends to cross a stream then ascends to meet a deep hollow way between trees, obviously part of a very old track.

    The Trail crosses this track through a hedge gap to rejoin it at the bottom then continues to follow it to a board indicating that the path is now diverted.

16. The new route is very clearly waymarked down to Barleighford Bridge; to the left of the bridge can be seen the hollowed approach to the earlier ford crossing the River Dane.

17. Follow the road, which also crosses a bridge over the feeder stream, back to the minor crossroads, retrace outward route back to the car park at Rushton Spencer.

Background Information

(1) Feeder Stream

Water is taken from the River Dane via the stream to feed nearby Rudyard Lake (1797), designed as a reservoir to feed the Leek Branch of the Trent and Mersey Canal.

(2) Wincle Grange

Once a monastic farm belonging to Combermere Abbey, Cheshire, parts of the building date to the fifteenth century. The gable end has an ecclesiastical look about it.

Walk 24	**Bearstone Rock (Roach End) - Forest Wood - Gradbach YHA - Three Shire Heads - Wildboarclough - Goosetree - Back Forest Ridge - Bearstone Rock.**
	(11 miles)
Description	**A walk of much scenic variety following old packhorse ways; splendid far ranging views throughout.**
Map	**OS Map Outdoor Leisure No. 24, scale 1:25000.**
Start	**Roadside at Roach End, ref. 996645.**

Route

1. Cross the wall stile at the top of the rough track, turn right to cross a second one, follow the path which descends to cross a little water course then ascends to the edge of Forest Wood.

2. Ignore the sign for Lud's Church (visit on return section), take the path straight ahead through the wood, keep left at a fork; later, at brook level, pass four-way signpost to reach and cross the footbridge over Black Brook.

3. Cross the nearby wall stile, follow riverside path to and through Gradbach YHA[1] grounds to the public car park along the road.

4. At the end of the car park go left over footbridge, follow river round the bend, cross wall stile right on to the roadway, turn right then left up a house drive.

5. Cross stile in right wall, follow left boundary over several fields, after crossing a ladder stile continue diagonally across field, follow curving wall to pass front of derelict building on to a track.

6. Follow this down to the beautiful but remote setting of Three Shire Heads, junction of the borders of Derbyshire, Staffordshire and Cheshire, also the crossing point of the River Dane for several packhorse ways.

    The original bridge has been widened as can be seen by looking under the arch.

7. Go over the bridge, follow the river upstream to a gate and a stile on its right.

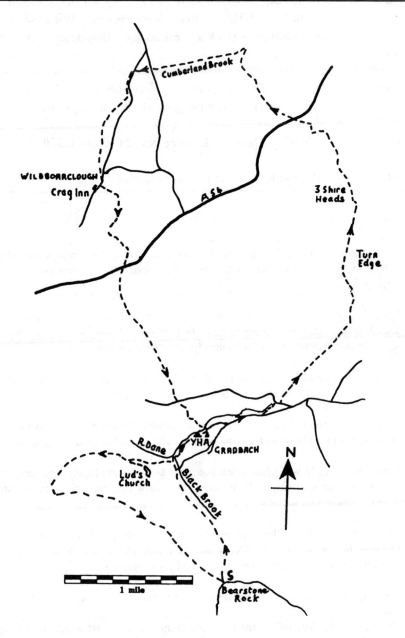

Cumberland Brook

WILDBOARCLOUGH
Crag Inn

A 54

3 Shire
Heads

Turn
Edge

R.Dane

YHA
GRADBACH

N

Lud's
Church

Black Brook

1 mile

S
Bearstone
Rock

Ignore the latter, continue ahead along a hollow way by field boundaries, after turning right through a gateway (farmhouse ahead) go left up the fields, cross two corner stiles on to the A54 (Macclesfield to Buxton).

8. Cross straight over on to a track descending gradually to the top of the tree-lined valley of the Cumberland Brook, continue descending on the path down the valley side to a roadway, go through the farmyard opposite, turn right and cross footbridge on to the road leading into Wildboarclough.

9. Climb the ladder stile opposite on to a wide green path which later, with the huge mound of Shutlingsloe (506m.) rising to the right, joins an access road, with views across the valley to Crag Hall and its fishing lake, which descends to the valley road through Wildboarclough[2].

10. Turn right along the road to a stile on left (The Crag Inn is a little further up the road), cross the stile and a footbridge, follow path to wall corner then go half right to a walled track which leads to a stile at corner of a wood.

11. Follow distinct path line past trees, diagonally down the field and past a derelict building, across the A54 on to a track through to the Algreave to Flash road.

   To the right is a house with the name 'The Eagle and Child'[3].

12. Go down the farm drive opposite, leave by stile at the bend, follow right boundary down the hill, then go left to a walled, partly paved track whch descends to Gradbach YHA via a footbridge.

13. Turn downstream to recross the footbridge over Black Brook, go right on the path signed *Swythamley*, rising through the wood to a footpath junction adjacent to a rocky outcrop, go left to visit Lud's Church[4], entrance adjacent to fenced area, then return to junction.

14. Continue across the open moor to a sign for Roach End and turn left to follow the ridge path back to the car.

Background Information

(1) Gradbach Youth Hostel

A one time silk mill; the walled, paved track from the footbridge was part of the packhorse route from this mill to the one at Wildboarclough.

(2) Wildboarclough

Turn left where the access road meets the valley road to see millworkers cottages and scant remains on site of the mill. Go right at the junction and just ahead on left is the former mill office building which, in recent times, housed the village sub post office but is now a private dwelling

(3) Eagle and Child

Eighteenth century inn built to serve packhorsemen; closed around 1920.

Eagle and Child is the emblem of the Stanley family (Lord Derby is the head) who still own Crag Hall.

(4) Lud's Church

A rocky chasm 200 ft. long by 60 ft. high caused by a landslip.

Used by 'Lollards' - followers of religious reformer John Wycliff, persecuted in reign of Richard II (1377-99).

'Lud' may derive from Walter de Ludank who held services here in fourteenth century.

Also suggested that Lud's Church is legendary Green Chapel where Sir Gawain fought the Green Knight in a return match following the earlier one at Camelot.

Walk 25	**Gradbach - Bennettsich - Parks - Wildboarclough - Hammerton Knowl - Wild Boar Inn - Hammerton Farm - Danebridge - Gradbach.**
	(9½ miles)
Description	**A walk of contrasts between open moorland and wooded valleys, giving a wide variety of views.**
Map	**OS Map Outdoor Leisure No. 24, scale 1:25000.**
Start	**Gradbach car park, ref. 999663.**

Route

1. Leave the car park on the waymarked path, cross the footbridge and follow river upstream, just beyond the bend cross stile right on to roadway.

2. Go left and, after crossing the bridge over the River Dane, take footpath on right at signpost just beyond Gradbach Wesleyan Chapel of 1849. The path climbs fairly steeply to join a farm road.

3. Follow right to second farmhouse, at footpath sign go left through gate along a track; where this turns keep ahead alongside wall and rejoin track.

4. Follow the track, which swings right past Parks (house) to its end at a gate, continue straight ahead on left of fence, then later right of fence, cross broken gate on to open moorland.

5. Keep straight ahead on a reasonably clear path line through a wall gap, a short way ahead the path gently curves right to meet a wall and a crossing path (stile in wall on right - checkpoint).

6. Turn left to reach and cross the roadway (A54) on to a clear path crossing another open moorland section; at its end go through gate and down track to roadway at Wildboarclough.

7. Turn right down the road to a junction, with Crag Hall[1] on right, go left here through a gate signed *Rottenstone Cottage*, follow the track past the cottage to Firs Farm at the track end.

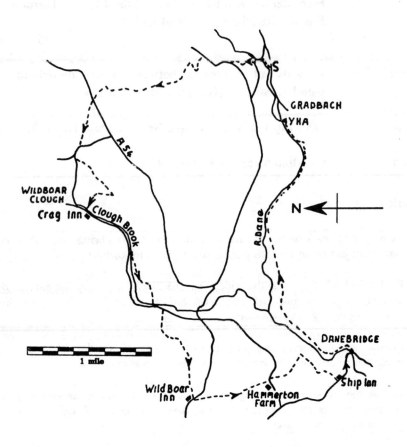

8. Go through the gate and straight on across the field to just short of a wall, turn back half right on another path (waymarker post ahead) to a wall outer corner, go left alongside wall on a stony track to cross a stile on edge of a wood, descend to roadway via footbridge and stile.

   In very wet weather the track becomes a stream, necessitating some detouring, evidence of which can be seen.

9. Follow the road left, past the Crag Inn, to the drive of Brookside Restaurant, cross the bridge and follow the footpath right, first alongside Clough Brook then

104

swinging left on to waymarked track.

10. Continue along the track to a signpost (*Wildboarclough, Owlers Bridge*) adjacent second of two barns, go down the field as directed and cross footbridge on to road.

11. Turn left then shortly right through a gate up a farm track which swings left to join the farm drive, continue along the drive to short of the trees, go right to a wall corner.

12. Ignore stile to right, follow wall uphill, cross stile, continue along boundary through a gateway then follow wall foundation and another boundary across two stiles, cross the next field on a diagonal to a stile and the road (A54) adjacent to the Wild Boar Inn.

13. Cross over to field entrance, ignore prominent stile on right, go over waymarked stile in curve of left wall, take a line a little right of electricity post directly ahead to reach a wall, keep left of this and follow through to a track which ends at the road above Wincle and the entrance to Hammerton Farm.

14. Turn left then right along another track, go right at the sharp bend, left at end of first building then right as waymarked.

15. After crossing a stile the path descends a little valley to cross a stream then ascends to another stile, go straight ahead past four-way signpost, through a 'kissing gate' and down steps opposite to the road adjacent to The Ship Inn above Danebridge.

    NB The steps drop directly on to the roadway with no preview of approaching traffic - exercise caution.

16. Continue down the road to the far end of the bridge, turn left on path for Gradbach which initially follows the river before swinging right to cross a stile.

17. The path ahead is easily followed as it rises through woodland with the river far below, followed by open moorland, then after passing a house, swings left to re-enter woodland and finally descends, after passing a path junction, to the footbridge at the confluence of Black Brook and the River Dane.

18. Cross the bridge and the stile ahead left, follow the path paralleling the river to the YHA[2], leave along the drive.

Note on the right the ancient stone water trough with seats either side where packhorse men would rest whilst their animals took the waters.

19. At the end of the drive go left along the road back to the car park.

Background Information

(1) Crag Hall

Belongs to the Stanley family, of which Lord Derby is the head.

Wildboarclough was once known as Crag - hence the name of the Hall and the Crag Inn.

(3) Youth Hostel   See Walk 24.

Walk 26	Ashford - Monsal Head - Upperdale - Water-cum-Jolly Dale - Miller's Dale - Brushfield - Great Shacklow Wood - Ashford.
	(9½ miles)
Description	Easy walking through picturesque dales of the River Wye with high level sections for longer distance views.
Map	OS Map Outdoor Leisure No. 24, scale 1:25000.
Start	Public car park (also toilets) in Ashford, ref. 194697.

Route

1. Leave the car park by the entrance, turn right up the Monsal Head road, take the path on the left by footpath sign, cross stile at the end, go through gate in far left corner of big field, straight ahead through another, then right on to a walled track.

2. Follow the track through to its end and turn left along field boundary; after crossing a stile, go right at the top on a well defined path through to Monsal Head, with fine views left along Monsal Dale, ahead to Upperdale and Longstone Edge over to the right.

   Although only a short distance covered, the location is worth a stop, with café, hotel, shops and public toilets available.

3. Where the road starts down to Upperdale cross stile left on a track down to the viaduct and the Monsal Trail[1], cross the viaduct, ignore left and right footpath accesses, carry on along the trail to its end near blanked off tunnel; continue along a hillside path finally crossing a footbridge at a weir adjacent to Cressbrook Mill[2].

4. A very pleasant riverside walk now follows, first through Water-cum-Jolly Dale, where the river was dammed and widened to form the mill pool, then Miller's Dale and Litton Mill[3].

5. Pass through the mill yard to the road, cross the river by the footbridge opposite the shop, to regain the Monsal Trail, but only for several yards to leave again

via stile on left.

6. The path climbs steeply up the hillside to meet a wall on the right; cross stile into a long narrow field, part way along left wall cross another stile and follow wall down the field to join a walled track.

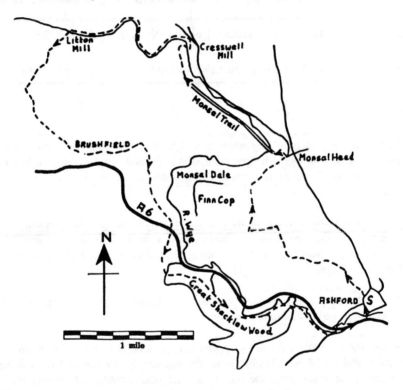

7. Follow the track left as it descends gently past Top, Middle and Lower Farms to a junction and signpost for *Brushfield Hough*, go right as directed, to a waymarked path descending steeply down the wooded hillside into Monsal Dale. Opposite and left is the flat top of Fin Cop, an Iron Age fort and settlement.

8. Turn right on the path which leads to the A6, cross with care to the car park and picnic area opposite, leave over the stile on pathway marked *2,3*; where these part company, follow *3* uphill and cross stile into Great Shacklow Wood.

9. The path, alongside which wild raspberries can be picked in season, passes through the wood, descending to the riverside where the tail (exit) of the Magpie Mine sough[4] can be seen discharging eight million gallons of water per day, clearly illustrating the drainage problems faced by the lead mines.

   To the right is the collapsed hillside which was blown out in 1966 by water pressure resulting from a complete blockage in the sough.

10. Further on is a disused mill with a two waterwheels set-up, once used for the making of bobbins for the textile industry. Also here can be seen pipes via which water was pumped, before mains water installation, to Sheldon 500 ft. above on the hilltop.

11. Where the riverside path reaches the roadway was another mill, used for polishing what was called Ashford Black Marble, which was, in reality, limestone full of bituminous impurities mined at the nearby Arrock Mine in Kirk Dale.

12. Go left along the road to the A6, cross right to re-enter Ashford[5] via Sheepwash Bridge[6] and so back to the car park.

Background Information

(1) The Monsal Trail

Track bed of the former LMS railway connecting Derby to Manchester via Miller's Dale and Chinley, completed in 1867. It ran through some of the most attractive scenery in Derbyshire.

Closed in 1960s under Dr Beeching's rationalisation programme.

(2) Cressbrook Mill

The original mill, built by Sir Richard Arkwright in 1785, was destroyed by fire in the same year.

Present mill by William Newton in 1815. An impressive Georgian structure powered by two large waterwheels, it was built for the spinning of cotton.

Newton was reputed for his humanity in his treatment of apprentice employees.

(3) Litton Mill

Original mill built in 1782 by Ellis Needham and partner, Thomas Frith. In 1803 employed 160 apprentices - orphans or paupers' children.

Needham acquired a reputation for brutality towards them on the basis of a document written by ex-apprentice Robert Blincoe. Subsequent research suggests Needham was too harshly judged.

The 1782 mill was completely destroyed by fire in 1874.

(4) Magpie Mine Sough

Made to 'unwater' (mining terminology) the Magpie Mine one mile away at Sheldon; took eight years in construction (1874-81) and cost approximately £35,000 against original estimate of £8,000. Proved to be fruitless.

(5) Ashford (Aisseford in Domesday Book - 'ford by the ashes')

The prehistoric Old Portway which traversed the Peak District, south-east to north-west, crossed the river in this vicinity some 4000 + years ago.

Church of 1870 incorporates the original Norman *tympanum* (space between lintel and arch) in the south door.

(5) Sheepwash Bridge

Seventeenth century packhorse bridge, so called because sheep were penned in the stone fold at the south end of the bridge prior to driving them across the river to wash their fleeces.

Walk 27	Winster Top - Limestone Way - Brightgate - Wensley - Watt's Shaft - Stanton Moor - Birchover - Winster Top.
	(9 miles)
Description	A walk rich in history of the lead mining era of seventeenth to nineteenth centuries, and Bronze Age man's burial grounds of 1500 BC on Stanton Moor. Extensive views along Derwent Valley.
Map	OS Map Outdoor Leisure No. 24, scale 1:25000.
Start	Parking area - side of minor road at Winster Top, ref. 240604.

Route

1. Follow the minor road to the white house, turn right at signpost, ascend hillside past Wyn's Tor Rocks to the walled track - Limestone Way.

2. Go left along the track to a wide gap in the left boundary, pass through half right (look for isolated stone stile) to join a path rising from Winster[1] village.

3. Continue on this path, cross stile, follow wall past Luntor Rocks, cross another then a third in boundary wall to carry on along other side of wall to a backward pointing waymark arrow.

4. Leave the wall on a diagonal straight line through four more stiles, follow direction arrow across field (wall removed), then diagonally again across large field to signpost and road.

5. Follow the road left to an S-bend (farmhouse right), cross stile left by gate, follow boundary right to second stile. *Do not cross*.

   The route now follows the Bonsall to Wensley miners' path.

6. Go half left, no visible path line, over the brow, pass two concrete gate posts, go through large wall gap below from where the path ahead can clearly be seen.

Also fine view down Derwent Valley towards Chatsworth

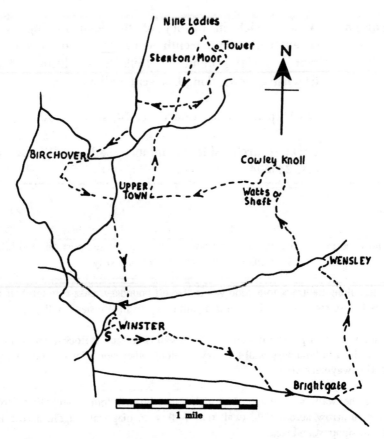

7. Descend the path with, all around, plentiful evidence of lead mining; at the same time, give a thought to the miners who trudged up and down this hill to and from the mines.

Shortly before the path makes final descent into Wensley Dale (route to Mill Close Mine), go left on a track to top of Wensley Dale, cross right on to another track up hillside into Wensley[2] past The Crown Inn.

8. Turn left up the road to stile on right just beyond Red Lion Inn, ascend the field alongside boundary, cross stile at top, descend steep path keeping left at a pond, to the valley bottom.

9. Follow path up to remains of Watt's Shaft[3] engine house, go right on track, cross stile/gate, follow track left up and round Cowley Knowl where it straightens *en route* to Birchover; this is the route followed by the miners from Birchover.

10. Where track bends left, cross stile right, follow field boundary to yard of Barn Farm, leave by stile/gate, cross stile in right corner on to road.

11. Go right then left across stile on to Stanton Moor[4], follow path to crossroads, turn right and shortly right again over fence stile on to path traversing edge of the moor.

    Fine viewpoint looking down left to Rowsley, Matlock right and Darley Dale near centre.

12. Follow the path to Earl Grey[5] Tower, take path left side to Nine Ladies[6] stone circle with the King Stone a little way left, leave on the broad path left side of the trees.

    On right just beyond trees is enclosure created by low, overgrown bank of stones with north and south entrances - remains of chambered cairn.

13. Continue, with evidence either side of other ruined cairns, to crossroads: left are the recognisable remains of a cairn. Turn right to the aptly named Cork Stone (like champagne bottle cork) then on to the road.

14. Go left to sharp bend, cross rough parking area (good views across to Elton, Youlgreave and Lathkill Dale area) to path descending through trees to roadside opposite Druid Inn, Birchover[7]. The Red Lion pub is left round the corner.

15. Take the path left of Druid Inn, with Rowtor Rocks[8] right and chapel left, cross stile at bottom left, climb narrow field on to Rocking Stone Farm drive, turn left, cross stile at end by gate.

16. Turn left, follow boundary path alongside Birchover Wood through to road at Upper Town Farm; old village stocks are a few yards away to left.

17. Turn right, descend lane to a bend, cross stile left on to what used to be a stone slabbed causeway; much of it is now grassed over although some sections have been reclaimed.

    Go through hedge gap at bottom of field, maintain same line following partly covered slabs, cross a little valley and hedge stile, continue left on paved way through two more stiles, go left side of the tree ahead to join the path across another small valley and hedge stile. The rest of the way is paved to join a track into the village of Winster.

    To the left is the old Market Hall, up the side street is the Bowling Green Inn.

18. Winster has many listed buildings some of which can be seen by turning right to pass the Hall, last used as a pub but empty at the time of writing, then left at the Dower House facing down the street.

    Where the road bends go left up a gennel or alleyway to the second right turn; before following the path, pause to look at the superb view across to Stanton Moor and across the Derwent Valley to Matlock Moor and others; go left at the fork and back to the car park.

    The section just covered illustrates vividly the way the village expanded during the boom years.

Background Information

(1) Winster (Winsterne in Domesday Book - 'Thorn Bushes')

Typical one street village until lead mining boom of eighteenth century; population 600 in 1676, 2000 by 1770.

Miners Standard (1653) was first inn, by 1770 there were 22 inns or alehouses.

There are 60 listed buildings, many built during eighteenthth century boom years. Market Hall dates from late seventeenth century when Winster was just a market town.

Other major buildings are:-

- **Hall** - recently a pub, was built mid-eighteenth century, original one was 1628.

- **The Dower House** - seventeenth century.

- **Two Chapels** - Primitive Methodist 1823, The Methodist 1837.

- **Church** - relatively young compared to most in Derbyshire, west tower 1721, the rest 1842, modification in 1883.

- A small stone building with a metal grille at the front and chute at the back stands at side of main road at Winster Top. This was **'The Ore House'** - overnight safe where miners left lead.

(2) Wensley (Wodnesleie in Domesday Book)

'Woden' in place name indicates pagan Anglo-Saxon settlement. Lead mining principal industry until around 1860.

(3) Watt's Shaft

Part of the Mill Close Mine (½ mile north) lead mining operations. Cornish engine (for pumping water out of the mine) house built 1859-60, abandoned 1874.

Mill Close Mine during 1930s was richest in country, but by 1938 5,500 gallons of water per minute were being pumped out to allow mine to be worked.

In same year, when two miles from shaft and 900ft. below River Derwent, underground lake breached - complete flooding of workings - mine abandoned.

(4) Stanton Moor

H. J. Massingham, nineteenth century newspaper editor, wrote, "Stanton Moor is as thick with tumuli as a plum duff with raisins". Between 1927 and 1950s some 73 burial cairns were uncovered to find human skeletons, beads, containers, flint and chert tools dating to 1500 BC.

(5) Earl Grey Tower

Memorial to Earl Grey's 1832 Reform Bill making parliamentary voting more democratic.

(6) Nine Ladies

The circle of 35 ft. diameter originally had small cairn in centre. Legend has it that nine ladies and a fiddler, the nearby King Stone, were turned into stone for dancing on the sabbath.

(7) Birchover (Barcovere in Domesday Book - 'birch-covered steep slope')

Once very active quarrying village, very little done these days.

Jesus Chapel founded early eighteenth century, rebuilt 1869, has interesting plaque commemorating Joan Waste, a 22 year old blind woman burnt at the stake, in Derby 1555, as a heretic.

(8) Rowtor Rocks

Once part of the estate of Revd. Eyre, founder of the chapel, who fashioned rough seats in the rocks with a stone access staircase so he and friends could sit and admire the view. Can be found at the top of rocks from path paralleling the track alongside.

Walk 28	Baslow - Baslow Edge - Curbar Edge - Froggart Edge - Haywood - Grindleford - Froggart - Calver - Curbar - Baslow.
	(10 miles)
Description	A walk of contrasts; gritstone edges, waterside paths and woodland. A popular area, choose a weekday or out of season to miss crowds.
Map	OS Map Outdoor Leisure No. 24, scale 1:25000.
Start	Bubnell Road, Baslow, ref. 252723.

Route

1. Leave Bubnell Road over the fifteenth century river bridge; note at the far end the small toll house/sentry box(?), with the entrance only 3½ ft high - probably due to the road level having been raised during the centuries since it was built.

   Turn right, cross the main road, noting to the right Baslow[1] church clock where the letters and numerals V I C T O R I A 1 8 9 7 replace the conventional arrangement. At the fork carry on up School Lane, keep left at the next junction on Baslow Bar ('bar' being the name given to a steep road from cliff edge to valley), a centuries old packhorse route.

2. Just short of speed derestriction sign, turn right by telegraph pole up a cul-de-sac, cross stile, follow path skirting top of wooded hillside which rejoins the Bar further up (eliminating a tedious rough ascent of which there is more ahead).

3. Once the top has been reached, with Wellington's Monument (1866) just ahead, an easy walk follows along the length of the Edges, with extensive views eastward over the moors, which contain much evidence of prehistoric man's presence, and westward over the Derwent Valley, showing the works of latter day man.

   Froggart Edge has numerous unfinished millstones lying about and, like Stanage Edge, is popular with rock climbers.

4. At the far end of Froggart Edge cross the road right, descend path across a

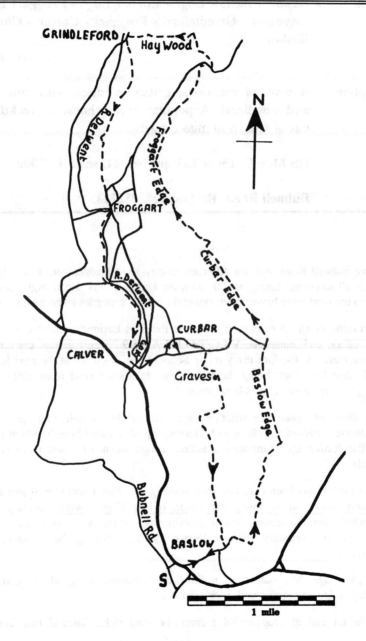

GRINDLEFORD

Hay Wood

N

R. Derwent

Froggatt Edge

FROGGART

Curbar Edge

R. Derwent

CURBAR

CALVER

Graves

Baslow Edge

Bubnell Rd.

BASLOW

S

1 mile

stream, continue ahead to cross a stile from where the path descends steeply through Haywood to join a farm track through to the road at Grindleford - a river crossing point of the eighteenth century Sheffield to Buxton turnpike.

The old Toll House is at the eastern end of the bridge.

5. Turn left to the bridge, left again on clear field path, cross footbridge and stile, turn right and cross stile into a delightful wooded section, rich with flowers in spring.

6. After leaving the wood, follow clear field path to join a walled track, which is a good example of a stone causeway, at the road keep straight ahead to Froggart Bridge spanning the River Derwent.

7. Cross the bridge and the stile on left, follow riverside path down to New Bridge, cross the road at the sharp bend, take path alongside the Goit (mill stream) to Calver Mill[2], which doubled for Colditz in the TV series of that name, and on to the road in Calver.

8. Cross the eighteenth century river bridge, turn left in front of the chapel on the road up to Curbar, take first left turn, Pinfold Hill, which ends opposite the original water supply system for the village.

9. Turn right then left uphill to a sign *Baslow via Gorse Bank Farm* at the drive entrance to Lane Farm, follow the drive to a cattle grid, go left through stile/gate and diagonally across the field and a stile on to a wide moorland path.

The circular building with a conical roof passed on the left was an eighteenth century short term jail.

10. Just ahead on the right are the Cundy graves, plague victims in 1632, 34 years before that which devastated the population of Eyam.

Follow the path through a small gate, then go right on narrow pathway through the bracken, cross stile/gate then another gate.

11. Go left across the field, pass through gateway and another half left to reach a track which continues through Gorse Bank farmyard on to Gorse Bank Lane,

ending at Baslow Bar.

12. Turn right, pass in front of Hawley's shop along Over Lane to rejoin School Lane back to Baslow village centre.

Background Information

(1) Baslow (Basselau in Domesday Book). Outlier of Ashford.

Village consists of three parts:-

- Bridge End, the original settlement at the river crossing,
- Nether End around the green and Bar Brook with several hotels, is the tourist centre,
- Over End, nineteenth century residential development along the A623, north of Bridge End.

Baslow Hall at Over End was built for Sebastian de Ferranti (1864-1930), founder of the electrical engineering company.

(2) Calver Mill (Calvoure in Domesday Book)

Present building dates from 1804 on site of earlier one destroyed by fire.

In 1833 the weir at Froggart Bridge was enlarged and a new goit constructed to feed two water-wheels, 24 ft. diameter and 17 ft. wide, in new stone housing at front of building.

Cotton spinning ceased 1923, building unused until World War II, became storage depot.

By 1947 was in state of decay, water-wheels gone for scrap; purchased by W. & G. Sissons of Sheffield for making stainless steel holloware.

Walk 29	Hathersage - North Lees - Green's House - Stanage Edge - Higger Tor - Carl Wark - Mitchell Fields - Hathersage.
	(8 miles)
Description	Splendid views and points of interest on this walk through 'Jane Eyre' country.
Map	OS Map Pathfinder 743 sheet, SK28/38, scale 1:25000.
Start	Public car park, Hathersage, ref. 232815.

Route

1. Leave the car park at the rear on footpath, past Rock Lea Activity Centre, to Hathersage[1] main street, go left of National Westminster Bank to end of narrow street, turn left as directed for the church which is reached by a dry weather footpath running uphill alongside a wall.

   In the churchyard is Little John's[2] grave, position indicated by sign board.

2. Leave through the gate, turn left and cross stile at footpath sign, turn left a short distance ahead, descend bank to cross stile and footbridge, some two thirds way up the hill go diagonally, pass through fence stile then cross another in far corner.

3. Continue alongside boundary to Cowclose Farm, follow drive to narrow lane, turn left then right on drive up to North Lees[3] Hall.

4. At the footpath sign by the house, go through the gate and along a broad path to a wood - *do not enter*; instead, turn back left on a grassy path, cross stile to continue on a well worn path to the site and ruins of a paper mill, an ideal picnic spot.

   En route, note the chapel ruins[4] in the fields to the left.

5. Leave along a clear path which, after crossing a field, joins a walled track to Green's House, cross the stile at the signpost, follow the track round the wall

corner where the path crosses to the other side of the wall before continuing to narrow road past Dennis Knoll.

The road was once the main route from Sheffield via Ringinglow to Bamford.

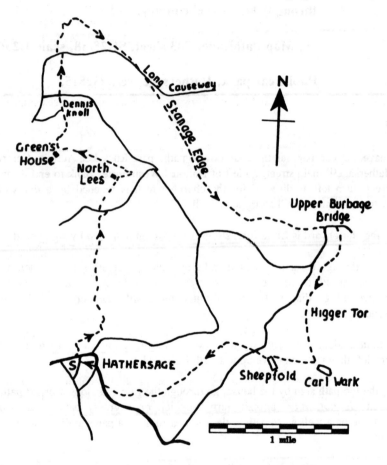

6. Cross straight over on a worn path (not shown on OS map) to a rough track, shown on the map as part of the Long Causeway[5], go left to cross stile on right, follow path uphill to its junction with another running parallel to Stanage Edge, turn right for some 50 yds or so to a narrow path through the heather heading at

about 45° to a 'break' where the top of the Edge is finally reached; many discarded millstones will be seen *en route*.

7. While following the path along the Edge, look out for the large boulders with man-made grooves and recesses to catch rainwater for the grouse, the water lying on the moors being too acidic. Each stone is numbered, there being 32 of them along the complete length of the Edge. Gamekeepers were responsible for filling them in dry weather.

Shortly after passing the trig point (457 metres), descend through the rocks on to a path leading to a road and Upper Burbage Bridge, a popular tourist stop.

8. Short of the bridge, cross the stile to follow the path along the west side of Burbage Brook valley to Higger Tor (high rock) then down and along to Carl Wark[6], which is worth climbing up to, if only to marvel at the huge stones used in the west defensive wall.

The entrance was on the south corner.

9. Return to the path, go back a few yards to a narrow path heading westward, follow this across the moorland, look ahead to a stone-walled sheepfold, the north wall of which is the target, follow the line of the wall through the small trees and descend to a roadway.

10. Cross the stile opposite to continue downhill to a house (Mitchell Field), go left then right as directed, cross two wall stiles then half left across the field on to a house drive.

11. At the bend carry straight on along a grassy path, later becoming a deep hollow way, descending steeply to join a metalled access road ending at the Sheffield road, turn right then first left to regain the car park.

Background Information

(1) Hathersage (Hereseige in Domesday Book)

One time centre of needle making industry.

In Charlotte Brontë's *Jane Eyre*, Hathersage equates to Morton. There was, in earlier days, a real Jane Eyre who lived at nearby Shatton Hall.

Eyre Chantry (1463) is north-east chapel in the church.

(2) Little John's Grave

Local tradition believes he was John Little, who fought with Simon de Montfort's army at Battle of Evesham (1265), outlawed after de Montfort's defeat.

Grave was opened in 1784 revealing a thigh bone 28 inches long, indicating a man some eight to nine feet tall.

(3) North Lees Hall

Built 1594-96, 'Marsh End' in *Jane Eyre*.

(4) Chapel Ruins

Built by the Roman Catholic Robert Eyre in 1685, connected by tunnel to North Lees Hall.

Chapel destroyed by Protestant mob in 1688.

(5) Long Causeway

Considered by some experts to be part of the Roman road from Navio (Brough) to Sheffield. Later experts believe the road crossed the edge approximately where this walk crosses it.

The rough road was certainly used as a packhorse route and, later, for the movement of the millstones.

(6) Carl Wark

Originally thought to be an Iron Age fort. Current thinking is that it dates around AD 500, builders unknown.

What did it protect, and from whom? - also unknown.

Walk 30	Eyam - Foolow - Abney Moor - Offerton Hall - Offerton Moor - Abney - Stoke Ford - Sir William Hill - Eyam.
	(11 miles)
Description	A mainly moorland walk along some old tracks and ways, excellent wide ranging views.
Maps	OS Map Outdoor Leisure No. 24; also required, Outdoor Leisure No. 1 and Pathfinder SK28/38 (all scale 1:25000).
Start	Eyam public car park, ref. 216767.

Route

1. Turn left from the car park, note on right spring-fed troughs of the old public supply system created in 1588 by the owner of Bradshaw Hall, the ruins of which are nearby.

   Go left down Eyam[1] main street, turn first right up New Close, a cul-de-sac, follow footpath between houses.

2. The way to Foolow is clearly defined and stiled. Cross two minor roads at beginning followed by numerous fields, some with evidence of leadmining, turn right in last field to the road at Foolow[2].

3. Go left to the village green with medieval cross, pond and well and intriguingly named pub, The Lazy Landlord, turn right along Bretton Road and cross stile left at a bend.

4. Follow wall, cross another stile, ascend hillside to Bretton-Great Hucklow road, cross stile opposite and descend steeply to a stream. Good break spot.

5. Cross the footbridge and stile ahead, cross second one in right wall, cross field to third stile in far wall and minor road adjacent to Abney Grange, in medieval times, a monastic farm owned by Welbeck Abbey, Nottinghamshire.

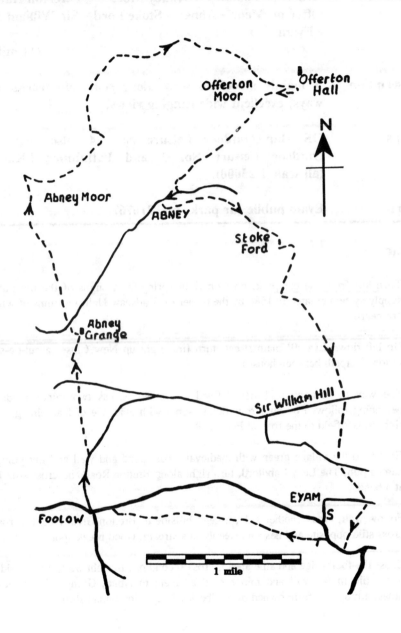

6. Turn left, then shortly right to cross stile on to a clear path for an exhilarating walk, with superb views, over Abney Moor, ending at a rough track, part of packhorse way, from Eyam to Brough and Bradwell.

7. Follow track right to wall corner, turn left as signed for Shatton, follow Shatton Lane (track) to 90° left hand bend, cross stile right on another distinct path across the contours of Abney Moor to Offerton Hall[3].

8. Cross stile onto path steadily ascending Offerton Moor, descend on far side to cross ladder stile seen ahead, turn left down field, cross two more stiles to road.

9. Turn right into Abney, left through gate by signpost (*via Stoke Ford to Eyam*), descend the delightful tree lined Abney Clough to the crossing of old packhorse ways at Stoke Ford (excellent spot for a break).

10. Cross the footbridge, take the path directly ahead for a short way, turn left on to hollow way, worn down by packhorses and men, then conventional path climbing the slope across two stiles on to Eyam Moor[4].

11. Ignore clear path left and one alongside trees right, instead take less distinct path, through the heather and a rock outcrop, to Sir William Hill[5], part of the 1757 Sheffield to Buxton turnpike.

12. It is now downhill all the way to Eyam.

    Cross the stile opposite, go straight down the fields, left are the remains of the Ladywash lead mine, to the Eyam-Bretton road.

13. Go half left, cross a stile, go diagonally left across two fields, continue on the path descending through the wood to another road.

14. Cross the stile opposite and one straight ahead in corner, turn left to follow the wall to its end, keep straight ahead on the path to the church and Eyam main street. Turn right to reach car park.

Background Information

(1) Eyam

Pronounced 'Eem' (Aiune in Domesday Book).

Saxon settlement of eighth/ninth century.

The actions and sufferings of the villagers during the plague of 1666 are well known and the plaques on cottage walls catalogue the tragic consequences.

Stocks can be seen on the village green.

Notable old buildings: Miners Arms (1630), Eyam Hall (1676), fine example of Derbyshire manor house, preceded by Bradshaw Hall.

Church - dates from thirteenth century, Saxon cross (eighth/ninth century) in churchyard is only one in Peak District to have retained its cross head.

Lead Mining - main industry during seventeenth/eighteenth century. Some spoil heaps and old veins in vicinity still worked for fluorspar, Ladywash Mine being one. Fluorspar is used as a flux in steelmaking and in ceramic and chemical industries.

(2) Foolow

Another centre of leadmining.

Foolow Hall (now two houses) with mullioned windows is seventeenth century.

Two-storeyed manor house with three-bayed facade is eighteenth century.

Among other old buildings, The Nook is seventeenth century,

Spread Eagle House (once an inn) is eighteenth century, church and chapel both nineteenth century.

Cross on village green is medieval but plinth Victorian.

(3) Offerton Hall

Sixteenth century origin, said to be one of seven halls built by Robert Eyre of Highlow Hall, one for each of his seven sons.

(4) Eyam Moor

Wet Withens, 100 ft. diameter, Bronze Age stone circle, other small ones and a few barrows.

Crossed by two packhorse routes, one NW via Stoke Ford, other NE via Hazelford (now Leadmill Bridge).

(5) Sir William Hill

The name dates back to at least 1692, at which time Sir William Saville was Eyam's Lord of the Manor and Sir William Cavendish owned Stoke Hall. Not known which one the hill was named after.

Walk 31	Eyam - Stoney Middleton - Froggart - Grindleford - Leadmill Bridge- Hazelford Hall - Stoke Ford - Mompesson's Well - Eyam.
	(10 miles)
Description	A mixture of riverside, woods and moorland.
Maps	OS Map Outdoor Leisure No. 24; also required Pathfinder SK28/38 (both scale 1:25000).
Start	Eyam public car park, ref. 216767.

Route

1. Turn left from the car park, note on right spring fed troughs of the old public supply system created in 1588 by the owner of Bradshaw Hall, the ruins of which are nearby.

   Go left down Eyam[1] main street to major road junction, go straight across to Lydgate[2] (right of café), follow this ancient way, past group of plague victims' graves and later, old parish boundary marker stone, through to minor road at Stoney Middleton[3].

2. Follow the minor road down past the church and the Bath[4] on left, to a bend, cross stile, take left path ascending slope to Knouchley Farm, go left round the buildings.

3. Leave by the drive, cross road and stile opposite, descend first field, cross into the second, follow River Derwent upstream to Froggart Bridge.

4. Cross bridge, turn left along road to sharp bend, go straight ahead on stone paved track, continue along clear field path, go through wood (colourful with wild flowers in spring and summer), cross stile then footbridge left, cross field on diagonal to Grindleford Bridge, built to carry Newhaven to Grindleford Turnpike; note toll house at eastern end.

5. Cross the road right to a footpath sign (Hathersage), follow path across two fields, turn left down boundary in third field, follow river for a pleasant walk through to Leadmill Bridge[5] near Hathersage.

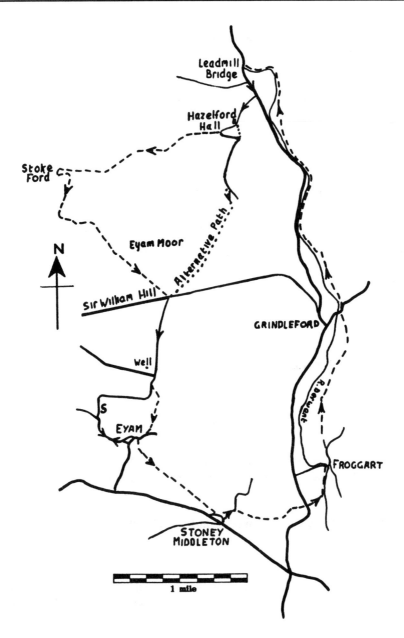

1 mile

131

6. Cross the bridge, take second right, a little used minor road, go past the seventeenth century Hazelford Hall* to an acute bend, keep straight ahead on a track to Tor Farm, keep ahead through gates on field path, pass through wood, cross a stream, ascend moorland path finally descending to Stoke Ford, junction of Highlow and Bretton Brooks and crossing of packhorse ways.

7. Do not cross footbridge, follow way to Eyam Moor[6] as Walk 35, on the moor take clear path left to follow boundary to junction of Sir William Hill and Eyam road.

8. Go down the road, visit Mompesson's Well[7] right near road junction, continue past junction to footpath sign left (no pointer), follow path descending through trees to join track into Eyam. Turn right through village back to car park.

   * From Hazelford Hall the walk can be shortened by 1½ miles, viz:-

   Go straight ahead up hillside path to rejoin road, continue ahead to footpath sign Sir William Hill, follow clear path across Eyam Moor to road junction as in 7.

Background Information

(1) Eyam   See Walk 30.

(2) Lydgate

Name derives from two old English words, 'llid' and 'geat' - swing gate. One time principal way into village; a watchman was posted at gate every night.

(3) Stoney Middleton (Middletune in Domesday Book)

(4) Bath

Leadmining centre since Roman times, Bath is legacy from these days, fed by thermal springs - constant temperature of 17°C. Renovated in nineteenth century by Lord Denman who owned the Hall of seventeenth century origin.

Church - Octagonal body of 1759 all pews face inward to centre, attached to fifteenth century tower.

(5) Leadmill Bridge

Built early eighteenth century, original stone arches widened in 1928; once called Hazelford Bridge, then on important trade route, Halifax Gate (road) for carrying Yorkshire wool and woollen goods.

(6) Eyam Moor   See Walk 30.

(7) Mompesson's Well

Named after William Mompesson, rector of Eyam during plague.

Outsiders brought supplies for the villagers, left them at various places around the village, the Well being one such place.

Villagers left money in the Well, immersed in vinegar, erroneously believing it to be a disinfectant.

Walk 32	Foolow - Silly Dale - Grindlow - Great Hucklow - Little Hucklow - Bradwell - Abney - Stoke Ford - Bretton - Foolow.
	(10 miles)
Description	Takes in several attractive villages with extensive and impressive views throughout.
Maps	OS Maps Outdoor Leisure Nos. 24 and 1, both scale 1:25000.
Start	Roadside by village green in Foolow, ref. 191768.

Route

1. Follow a narrow walled track signed *Silly Dale*, from far left corner of village pond, pass through gate and small one nearly opposite.

2. Go half right, cross four clearly stiled fields on a straight line, cross next two on diagonal to reach walled track, cross over, go half left across three fields to rejoin track.

3. Immediately turn right on to another track along Silly Dale, (possibly so called because of its puny size compared with other dales), at the end follow road through Grindlow[1], go left at road fork to stile right at end of a garden.

4. Cross garden and corner stile, follow stiled path alongside boundary to road at Great Hucklow[2].

5. Turn right, then left, follow main street to just beyond Queen Anne pub, turn right and follow rough track to Bradwell road.

6. Go up the road opposite into Little Hucklow with the Old Bull's Head Inn incorporating part of the Old Hall bearing date 1661. The inn has large collection of leadmining and farming relics.

7. Just past the inn, at a wall corner, turn right on to walled track, cross stile at far end, go straight ahead, cross another in field left corner, follow track to road.

8. Turn right to barn corner, go left on track, cross waymarked stile right by a gate, follow boundary and on a straight line, cross six more waymarked stiles, then go half right, cross stile by gate on to narrow lane.

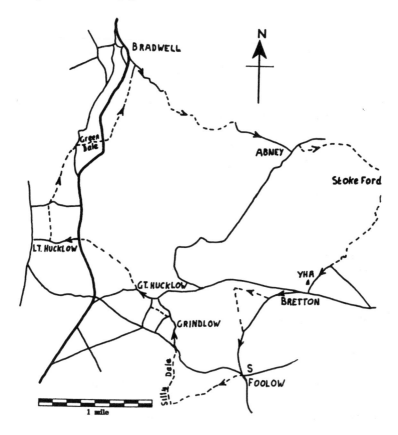

9. Follow the track opposite, down Green Dale to the Bradwell road, cross over on to signed path alongside farm buildings, at signpost turn part left, follow straight line up field between old mine workings spoil heaps, descend and cross stile on to one of Bradwell's[3] many side streets.

10. Go down the street to the Green (left down the steps is a café - walkers welcome), turn right down Bessie Lane, keep left to fork of two tracks.

135

11. Take one right, signed, very faintly, for *Abney*, keep right at a junction, join footpath raking steeply up the hillside, keep right again at fork, cross stile at top, follow boundary wall, join rough track, a packhorse route down to Brough.

12. Turn right along the track, right again down narrow lane into Abney[4], go left to footpath sign right (*via Stoke Ford to Eyam*), follow track down picturesque Abney Clough to Stoke Ford, good picnic spot.

13. Cross the footbridge, keep straight ahead on distinct path, pass through a small wood, swing left by a fence, cross stream.

14. Follow the steep path through hairpin bends and zig-zag, at top bear right, cross stile, follow walled track to road at Nether Bretton.

15. Continue up road to Barrel Inn at Bretton, turn right along road, then left signed *Foolow*, at a bend go right on a path to intersection with another climbing hilliside.

16. Turn left down hill, cross stile, follow field boundary, join road back to Foolow[5].

Background Information

(1) Grindlow

An ancient settlement with a prehistoric round barrow.

(2) The Hucklows (Hochelai in Domesday Book)

Once centres of leadmining dating back to eleventh century. Main activity nowadays is fluorspar extraction for use in chemical and steel industries.

Camp Hill, north of Great Hucklow is site of Gliding Club; has been used for World Championships.

(3) Bradwell (Bradewelle in Domesday Book)

Also an ex-leadmining centre, now associated with quarrying and the nearby cement works.

Famous, at one time, throughout the Peak, for the 'Bradder Beaver' a hard felt hat for lead miners; seven factories occupied in making them in their 'heyday'.

Bagshawe Cavern, discovered 1800 (original proprietor Sir William Bagshawe), is entered after descent of 130 steps. Contains beautiful crystallisations and stalactites.

The Old Bowling Green Inn is sixteenth century.

(4) Abney (Habenai in Domesday Book)

1750 birth place of William Newton, 'The Poet of the Peak'; his verses denouncing barbaric gibbeting at nearby Wardlow Mires created such a public outcry it became the last in England.

(5) Foolow   See Walk 30.

Walk 33	Castleton - Lose Hill - Hollins Cross - Mam Tor - Rushup Edge - Barber Booth - Hollins Cross - Castleton.
	(11 miles)
Description	Considered by many to be the finest ridge walk in the Peak District and consequently very popular. Superb views over Hope and Edale Valleys, plus the attractive and interesting village of Castleton.
Map	OS Map Outdoor Leisure No. 24, scale 1:25000.
Start	Public car park in Castleton, ref. 149829.

Route

1. Leave the car park along the footpath beside the stream, turn left along the minor road later becoming a track, keep right at the fork past Hollowford Training Centre, leave at a bend by signpost for Lose Hill.

2. Follow similar sign directions to a track alongside Lose Hill Hall[1]; at end of hall boundary wall, cross stile on to waymarked path (white or yellow painted poles) alongside drainage channel, cross footbridge after second stile, continue past poles on to a track.

3. At its end, cross waymarked stile and three others similarly marked, turn left and cross ladder stile then veer right to a two-way signpost on hillside and the path from Hope rising to the ridge.

4. The path climbs steadily to Lose Hill then more steeply to the hilltop (also known as Ward's Piece[2]) at 1563 ft. After a slight descent Back Tor is reached. There is a sheer drop at the back edge; keep well to left on the path, especially in poor visibility.

5. Continue along the well worn ancient way to Hollins Cross[3] and up to Mam Tor[4] at 1695 ft., then descend the stepped path (erosion repair), cross a narrow road and ascend to Rushup Edge.

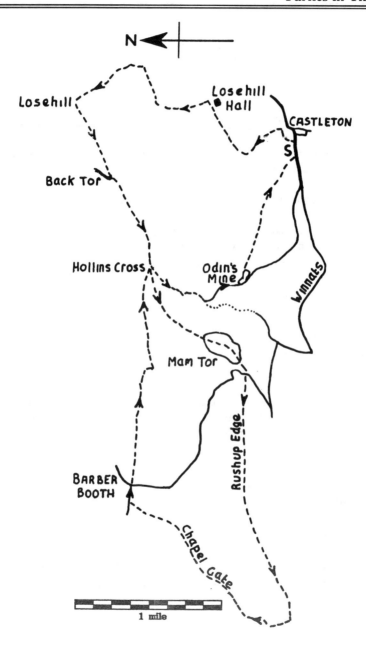

N

Losehill

Losehill Hall

CASTLETON

S

Back Tor

Winnats

Hollins Cross

Odin's Mine

Mam Tor

Rushup Edge

BARBER BOOTH

Chapel Gate

1 mile

6. Here are two adjacent paths, one on the ridge, the other below on the south side, the latter being the one used by travellers centuries ago to escape the force of the north winds.

   Take the ridge path past Lord's Seat (Bronze Age tumulus) at 1800 ft. to its junction with Chapel Gate ('gate' from Scandinavian 'gata' - road), an ancient route, later used by packhorse trains from Chapel-en-le-Frith. Turn right as directed for Edale via Barber Booth on a deeply worn path descending steeply (keep ahead at a left turn by a post) to a stile/gate at the bottom, then immediately cross wall stile left on to a clear field path over several stiles descending more gently past Manor House Farm to a narrow lane at Barber Booth[5].

7. Turn right to the road junction, take the footpath signed *Castleton, Hollins Cross and Hope* which is clearly waymarked every few hundred yards until it drops down to an access road, here turn right uphill to a stile by signpost for Hollins Cross and Castleton, cross on to a track which rakes steadily up the hillside to Hollins Cross.

8. Take the path from the Cross that leaves half right and descends to the drive of Mam Farm, follow through to what is left of the A625, go left down to Odin's Mine[6], right of the road and the 'crushing circle' on the left which is reached via a small gate.

9. Follow the path past the circle across a footbridge then descend to the drive of Knowlegates Farm, cross straight over on to a field path, clearly defined on the ground and also by yellow paint on stiles, which leads back to Castleton[7] (turn left to the car park).

Background Information

(1) Lose Hill Hall

Residential study centre operated by the Peak Park Board, offering a wide range of courses incorporating outdoor activities.

(2) Ward's Piece

G. H. B. Ward (1876-1957) was a Sheffield man who campaigned tirelessly for public access to the moors. In 1900 he founded Sheffield Clarion Rambling Club, claimed as the first active one in Britain.

His many friends bought the summit of Lose Hill and presented the deeds to G. H. B. in April 1945 in appreciation of his life's work.

2000 ramblers were present and at the same ceremony he handed over the deeds to the National Trust.

(3) Hollins Cross

For centuries this was the point at which the Edale to Castleton way crossed the ridge; it was the route by which coffins were carried to Castleton for burial prior to 1634, at which date Edale had its own consecrated chapel.

(4) Mam Tor (Mother Mountain)

Known as the Shivering Mountain on account of instability resulting from its being composed of bands of shale - these strata being clearly seen on the south side, exposed following a massive landslip in the 1970s, virtually destroying a section of the A625 road which has remained closed and abandoned.

At 16 acres, and with double ramparts, Mam Tor is the largest Iron Age fort in the Peak District and bears evidence of earlier, Bronze Age occupation.

(5) Barber Booth

One of five 'booths' in the Edale Valley, they were originally enclosed farms for protection against wolves.

(6) Odin's Mine and Crushing Circle

Suggested, because of its name, to have been associated with the Danes, but no evidence exists of it having been worked until the seventeenth century; closed in 1847.

Lead ore was placed on the circular iron track and crushed by the large wheel operated by horse power. An illustration of the mechanism can be seen in the Information Shop at Castleton.

(7) Castleton (most surprisingly not recorded in The Domesday Book)

A fine example of a medieval village; the layout is still that of the twelfth century 'planners'.

Originally a Saxon settlement with a fortification on the site now occupied by Peveril Castle.

Peveril Castle was built in 1076 for William Peveril, a favourite of King William the Conqueror (and not, as many suggest, his illegitimate son). Henry II added the keep in 1176.

Castleton and the whole Royal Forest was governed from the castle, whose greatest period was from the twelfth to fourteenth century, although it was still in use in fifteenth century as a hunting lodge; by the seventeenth century it was in ruins.

Beneath Castle Hill is Peak Cavern with a semi-circular entrance some 50 ft. high and 100 ft. wide.

A rope walk can be seen inside the entrance where rope-making took place from the fifteenth century up to 1967.

Also in the cave mouth up to the beginning of this century were workers' cottages; an account of 1794 reported there also being an inn.

Guided tours of the Peak Cavern are available, as is the case with the nearby Speedwell and Treak Cliff Caverns.

Walk 34	Castleton - Lose Hill Hall - Lose Hill Farm - Townhead - Bagshaw Bridge - Win Hill Pike - Aston - Hope - Castleton.
	(10 miles)
Description	Another fine walk in the area, part moorland with great views over the Woodlands Valley and Ladybower Reservoir to the moors beyond, and a finish through water meadows.
Map	OS Map Outdoor Leisure No. 24, scale 1:25000.
Start	Public car park in Castleton, ref. 149829.

Route

1. Start as Walk 33, sections 1 to 3. On reaching the Hope to Lose Hill path, turn right and cross stile beyond farm, ignore stile right, continue straight on as indicated by signpost for Hope. Win Hill Pike can be seen ahead on the horizon. Later the path joins a hollow track which descends to an access road to Townhead.

2. Turn left, then left again at *Bed & Breakfast* sign on to another access road, follow through to Oaker Farm, leave on a narrow footpath which later becomes wide and grassy, swinging round the slope. Cross a ladder stile on to a track, follow under railway bridge (carrying the Hope Valley section of the Sheffield to Manchester line), to Edale road.

3. Cross right to gate by signpost, descend bank and cross Bagshaw Bridge over the River Noe, follow the road to Edale End. Coffee and tea are available at Carr House Farm. Turn right as signed for Hope Cross and Jaggers Clough, go left after the gate then right at the wall corner.

4. The route climbs steeply (easy going after this) to a junction with a hollow way.

   The hollow way, once on the Roman road from Melandra Fort, near Glossop, to Navio, the Roman fort at Brough, or to join Batham Gate (another Roman road) at Bradwell, later became known as Doctor's Gate (road)[1].

5. Turn right, but not down the hollow way; instead, take the clear path left to follow the tree line at the top of Woodlands Valley.

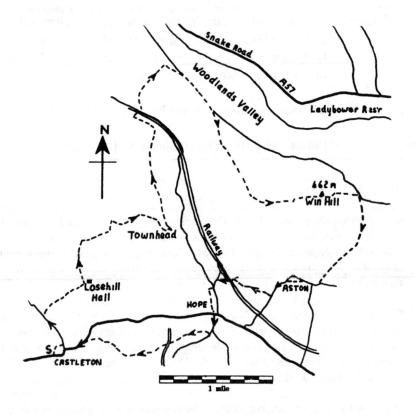

After crossing another path rising up the hillside and into the wood, a very narrow path forks left to Win Hill; this is a concessionary route but is little more than a rut through the heather and is not easy walking.

The preferred route is to take the left fork a little further on which carries through to the Pike.

The views from the top are superb, look north to Howden Moors then, moving eastwards, take in the rocky pile of Back Tor silhouetted on the skyline, round to

Derwent Edge and Moors. Stanage Edge lies to the east, with Offerton Moor round in the south.

6. Leave the Pike on the far side down a rutted path across twin ladder stiles then steeply down to a wall side, swing right, ignore stile left, on a very good path along the hillside.

7. Just beyond a water trough the path forks, go through the gap at a wall corner on an easy path gently ascending through the heather before dropping to cross a ladder stile.

8. Continue downhill alongside the trees, cross stile at the next row of trees and descend to a lane at Aston.

9. Turn right, go past the Hall (1578) and the road junction, to where the lane crosses a stream, leave here on a footpath to rejoin the road round a bend, follow to Farfield Farm drive.

10. Go along the drive, keep left at the farm entrance, pass under railway bridge, turn left to cross bridge over the River Noe to join Edale road.

11. Cross straight over the road and three stiles in line up a field, turn left at the Lose Hill signpost, follow the boundary through to small housing estate, maintain the same line but, using the footpath, pass through two 'kissing' gates to reach the main road through Hope[2], café a few yards right.

12. Opposite is Pindale road with the church on left; go up the road, noting the pinfold[3] near the bridge, pass the Bradwell turn, then turn right at signpost for Castleton on a clear path through the meadows of Peakshole Water - the stream emanating from Peak Cavern, Castleton; turn left along the road to reach the car park.

Background Information

(1) Doctor's Gate

A mention of Doctor Talbot's Gate first appeared in 1627. Dr John Talbot, illegitimate son of the Earl of Shrewsbury, was vicar of

Glossop (1494-1550). He probably used the route when visiting his father's castle in Sheffield.

(2) Hope (Hope in Domesday Book)

Stands on an isthmus between River Noe and Peakshole Water.

Fourteenth century church has a Norman font and part of a ninth century Saxon cross in the churchyard adjacent to the porch.

(3) Pinfold

An enclosure where stray animals were 'pinned' (penned) until claimed by their owner on payment of a fine. The person in charge of the pinfold was the 'pinder'.

(4) Castleton   See Walk 33.

Walk 35	Monsal Trail - Chee Dale - Mosley Farm - Tunstead - Hargatewall - Peter's Dale - Wormhill - Monsal Trail.
	(9 miles)
Description	Chee Dale is one of Derbyshire's most delightful dales; the River Wye, normally placid, in parts has characteristics of mountain stream, Peter's Dale full of wild flowers in spring, Wormhill an attractive village.
Map	OS Map Outdoor Leisure No. 24, scale 1:25000.
Start	Public car park at Millers Dale Station on Monsal Trail, ref. 137733.

Route

***Warning! This walk should not be attempted at times of high water when the stepping stones (see paragraph 3) may be submerged.

1. Turn right from the car park along the Monsal Trail[1], past a disused lime kiln, to a bridge over the River Wye, leave right, descend steps to riverside.

2. Follow the river up to Wormhill Springs, cross footbridge, continue on path, with the impressive rock faces of Chee Dale either side of the river, to a footbridge.

3. Cross over, turn right along opposite bank for a short distance, recross to north bank, continue on the riverside path, in two places replaced by stepping stones, which at times of high water will be impassable***.

4. After going under a railway bridge, the path is bordered by stone wall, cross stile at end, follow track back right under another railway bridge which carried the mineral railway to Great Rocks Dale Quarry[2].

5. Follow the zig-zag path up to Mosley Farm, turn left from centre of farmyard on to walled track through to a road, turn right for Tunstead. In roadside field on left short of Taylor Farm is a plaque to mark birthplace of England's first great

canal engineer, James Brindley (1716-72)[3].

6. A little further on, turn right down farm track, cross stile in field far right corner, then straight ahead across second, past a tumulus right, to a roadway.

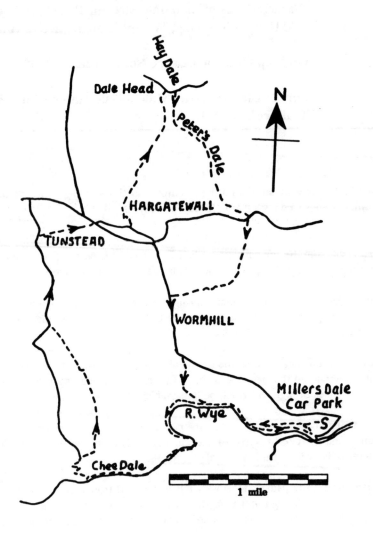

7. Cross straight over on the lane down to the hamlet of Hargatewall, turn left at the bottom on minor road, past large farm buildings to a crossing of tracks: note gate posts with initials 'RW'[4].

8. Follow track right to second left turn, go ahead along boundary of two fields, cross stile in facing wall, the clear path descends to a narrow lane at the junction of Hay Dale and Peter's Dale.

   Rocks at end of former make an excellent lunch spot.

9. At far end of Peter's Dale, cross road right to stile, follow steeply ascending path, turn right at top, then right at a fork, through to road at Wormhill[5].

10. Walk through the village past the stocks, Brindley's Well and a tea-room (very friendly welcome), to a sharp left bend. Seventeenth century Wormhill Hall is to left and a little way on is a donkey sanctuary.

11. Opposite the sanctuary is a narrow, signposted track; follow this as it descends back down into Chee Dale, continue all the way downstream to just short of roadway, cross stile left, ascend path back to Monsal Trail and car park.

Background Information

(1) Monsal Trail

Track bed of LMS railway line which connected Derby to Manchester via Millers Dale and Chinley. Completed in 1867, closed 1960s by Dr Beeching's rationalisation programme.

A very scenic route through some of the most beautiful areas of the Peak District.

(2) Great Rocks Dale Quarry

The largest in the world outside the USA, producing annually five million tons of exceptionally pure limestone - 98% calcium carbonate. Quarry face 1½ miles long.

(3) James Brindley

Although more or less illiterate throughout his life, was largely responsible for 350 miles of canals built during eighteenth century.

A first class engineer and innovator, also created engineering systems for textile mills including Lower Crag Mill, Wildboarclough.

(4) 'RW'

Initials of a Mr Whitehead, owner of Stanton and Staveley ironworks earlier this century. A shire horse breeder and exhibitor (large buildings were stables), he used to hire a complete train to take his entourage and horses to the major shows.

(5) Wormhill (Wruenele in Domesday Book)

The well on the village green commemorates James Brindley and is 'dressed' late August.

St Margaret's Church was rebuilt in 1864 but the tower base dates from 1273. Two things set it apart from other Peakland churches:-

1. It has a peal of miniature bells made as models at a Loughborough foundry,

2. The tower has a steep pitched cap inspired, according to Sir Nikolaus Pevsner, by the Rhineland Romanesque style or by the famous Saxon tower at Sompting in Sussex.